Encouragers:
The Sunday School Worker's Counseling Ministry

Encouragers:

THE SUNDAY SCHOOL WORKER'S COUNSELING MINISTRY

James E. Taulman

BROADMAN PRESS
Nashville, Tennessee

Unless otherwise indicated, Scripture quotations are from the King James Version of the Bible. Scripture quotations marked (GNB) are from the *Good News Bible,* the Bible in Today's English Version. Old Testament: Copyright © American Bible Society 1976; New Testament: Copyright © American Bible Society 1966, 1971, 1976. Used by permission. Scripture quotations marked (RSV) are from the Revised Standard Version of the Bible, copyrighted 1946, 1952, © 1971, 1973.

Dewey Decimal Classification: 268.3
Subject Headings: SUNDAY SCHOOLS // COUNSELING
Library of Congress Catalog Card Number: 85-19523
Printed in the United States of America

Library of Congress Cataloging-in-Publication Data

Taulman, James E., 1937-
  Encouragers : the Sunday school worker's counseling ministry.

  Bibliography: p.
  1. Counseling. 2. Encouragement—Religious aspects—Christianity. 3. Sunday-schools. 4. Sunday-school teachers. I. Title.
BV1523.C6T38 1986   253.5   85-19523
ISBN 0-8054-3712-6 (pbk.)

CONTENTS

TO
all those hurting people
who trusted me enough to share
a part of themselves with me

Foreword

The Sunday School worker is nearer to the griefs, pains, fears, aspirations, hopes, temptations, transgressions, and personal decision making of people than most people in the churches. You have face-to-face, day-to-day access to people at the moment of their crises. You are their "son or daughter of encouragement," as Jim Taulman has placed you in company with Barnabas, one of the most important biblical heroes. People are discouraged, disheartened, and cast down under the many stresses they carry. You can draw on the power of "the God of steadfastness and encouragement," of whom Paul speaks in Romans 15:5 (RSV), and in turn become an "encourager" of those in your Sunday School who need you.

Jim Taulman provides you specific, reliable wisdom in the work of encouragement. His vivid description of this lively ministry will bring new enthusiasm to your work when you are weary in well doing. His illustrations are so accurate and true to life that you will find yourself visualizing specific people like those whom he describes. Yet he describes them with such considerateness and understanding that you will experience a new compassion and learn a deeper wisdom for those of whom you are reminded.

You will find nothing stilted or awkward in his recommendations to you, but you will find a natural easiness that gives you confidence to take hold of the concerns people present you or which you sense on your own. In a very important pattern of ways, Jim Taulman *is* an encourager to both you and me as we read his book. I commend it to you with a whole heart as a reservoir of wisdom, guidance, and encouragement for you in your very necessary task as a Sunday School worker.

WAYNE E. OATES, Ph. D.
Professor of Psychiatry and Behavioral Sciences
Director, Program in Ethics and Pastoral Counseling
University of Louisville School of Medicine
and
Senior Professor of Psychology of Religion
Southern Baptist Theological Seminary
Louisville, Kentucky

1
The Ministry of Encouragement

By his encouragement, he gave the world one of the greatest theological minds it has ever known. By his encouragement, he gave the world the first written Gospel. By his encouragement, he gave the world more than three fourths of the New Testament. By his encouragement, he led the early church to share their physical resources with each other. Who was he? His name was Joseph, but he was renamed "One who Encourages" (Acts 4:36, GNB) or Encourager, or as we have come to know him, Barnabas.

Nearly every time we encounter Barnabas in Acts, he is engaged in encouraging and strengthening people. We first meet him when he sold some property and gave the proceeds to encourage the struggling church (Acts 4:36-37). He encouraged Paul after Paul's conversion when all of the other apostles were afraid to have anything to do with Paul (Acts 9:26-27). He enlisted Paul to come to Antioch to help him in the work of preaching and evangelizing (Acts 11:25-26). We encounter him again when he and Paul had a difference over whether John Mark should accompany them on a second missionary journey. Paul refused because Mark had turned back for some reason during their first journey. Barnabas, seeking to encourage Mark, let Paul select another companion, and Barnabas took Mark with him, thereby saving Mark for his task of writing the Gospel (Acts 15:36-40).

It is a sobering thought to realize that Barnabas influenced Mark and encouraged him in the faith. He encouraged Paul when no one else would trust him. Paul in turn influenced Luke. When Mark's Gospel, Luke's Gospel and Acts, and all of Paul's letters are added together, they compose well over three fourths of the New Testament. This is a significant impact for one man to make. And he did it by encouraging people!

9

Encouragers have been needed from the earliest days of the church. They are still needed today. People often come to a particular point in their lives and find an insurmountable obstacle. Much of the time they only need a little encouragement to get over the hurdle. They need someone to believe in them. They need someone to speak a word of encouragement to them. They may need someone just to listen as they lay out their options.

All Christians can and should be encouragers. However, one group has a built-in advantage already: Sunday School workers. The average Sunday School worker comes in contact with people who need help and encouragement almost daily. Most people respect the position of the Sunday School worker. Workers can be encouragers in the finest sense of the word. They touch people's lives that the average minister does not touch. They often encounter needs before the pastor does. Sunday School workers are a first line of defense.

Surrounding the northern part of the North American continent is what once was called a DEW line—a Defense Early Warning system (now called White Alice) designed to detect at the earliest possible moment an attack from over the North Pole area.

In a far different sense, Sunday School workers are an early warning system in detecting the needs and problems of members of Sunday School classes. Sunday School workers are a first line of defense. They have the opportunity to touch lives before most others in the church do. This emphasizes the importance of the role of Sunday School workers as counselors. In a properly functioning class, a teacher or worker will be in regular contact with members of the class. They will know when some of the first warning signals appear. They will be able to come to the aid of persons before problems have developed beyond a point of no return. They will be able to provide support and concern to a couple who have lost a child. They will be able to provide encouragement to a recent divorcee. They will be able to provide support and referral to an alcoholic or drug abuser. They will be able to help a teenager who feels so isolated from family and friends that suicide begins to look attractive.

Especially is this true in larger churches where the pastor and/or staff cannot possibly come in contact with all of the members on a regular basis. However, Sunday School workers who are in a small class, who take seriously their responsibility to care for and minister to the members of their class or group, are in touch with their members on a regular basis. If they have made the effort to get to know their members outside the classroom, they will already have built a rapport with the class members. When needs or crises come, the bridge is already built. An opportunity is already present to minister and provide help and encouragement.

The Need for Counseling

The need for counseling today is greater than ever. The stresses and tensions in our society are tremendous. They affect every household. No one is exempt.

Many serious problems exist in people's lives. Statistics now indicate that divorce directly affects nearly one and a quarter million people each year.[1] One third of our nation can be classed as moderate to heavy drinkers.[2] One recent study showed that 38 percent of the girls in our nation will be sexually abused by the time they are eighteen years old.[3]

The tensions are also present in many smaller ways as well. The regular activities that occur in our normal lives are all a part of the stress that we experience. People move regularly, they lose their jobs, they have children who grow up and leave home, illness strikes, parents and other family members die. These unavoidable experiences of life cause constant stress which can lead to either physical or mental illness or both.

Many of these problems are serious enough to disrupt totally the person's normal life pattern. One's sleeping or eating habits may change; arguments between spouses may increase; one may withdraw from regular activities.

In the case of Sunday School members, they may drop out of Sunday School completely, or at best, attend only infrequently. Why? They may be embarrassed by their circumstances. They may be angry at God for allowing a tragedy to strike them. They may feel their church does not approve of them under their present circumstances.

Several years ago, I attended a Wednesday evening service of a church that had a reputation of being a strong Bible-teaching church. At the beginning of the service, the pastor informed the congregation that two of their members had been involved in a traffic accident.

One insurance company was suing the other. In order to keep from bringing any discredit on the church, the women had requested that their names be removed from the church roll.

I have thought of this experience many times over the years. I admire the women's concern for not wanting to bring dishonor on their church. Would that more people felt that way!

However, at the time of a great need in their lives, the women were denied the support of their church. Where would one draw the line? What problems would constitute a need to remove one's name from the church roll? Would a divorce? A child who had difficulties with the law? A spouse jailed for failure to pay income taxes? How about just a marital separation? Or a child who broke the law but was not prosecuted? Or a spouse who cheated on his income taxes but was not caught?

Sunday School workers are concerned with ministry to people. They will seek to support and encourage people during times of stress and conflict rather than pulling out from under them what should be a primary means of support: their church. Workers will be more concerned with people than with the reputation of the church. The early church had several members who had been arrested and served time in prison. Paul and Silas were just two of them.

People are hurting. People in our Sunday School classes have problems. People who are active church members experience stress. To help relieve some of this stress, Sunday School workers can learn to read some of the early warning signs of hurt and pain and, in some cases, help to deter or diffuse an attack. Many times people need only to hear a word of encouragement or to have someone believe in them. Sunday School workers can become encouragers. Like Barnabas, they may be able to salvage someone who will be valuable in the Lord's work in the future.

Teachers who have taught Sunday School classes for any length of time have had some person come to them and share some particular need or problem. The problem might be a need for spiritual guidance. It might be a request for help in how to get along with a particular member of the family or a neighbor. It might be a question about a troubled marriage or a serious moral problem.

As the worker and class member talk, a counseling session is in progress. This may occur while walking down the hall on the way to the worship service. It might be over lunch. It might be in a home or office.

Sunday School workers have a unique relationship with their class members. Often they will have the opportunity of touching the lives of their members before any other professional counselor does. This places workers in an important position. Many times they can offer a word of information or a word of encouragement, and the need will be met. On other occasions they will have to spend more time in helping the troubled person find the answer. Then, in some situations, the worker will need to refer the person to someone else who has more skill in a particular area.

In all of these situations, Sunday School workers have a unique opportunity of helping people meet the needs created by the complex way we live. This is teaching in the fullest sense of the word. It is also counseling in the fullest sense of the word. The basic premise of this book is that Sunday School workers are counseling on a regular basis. Workers need to recognize and accept this counseling ministry, and to learn how they can better minister to their members and potential members.

Do You Want to Counsel?

This is a valid question that each worker in the Sunday School must answer. Some answer it in the negative. They feel counseling is not for them.

This is fine. The purpose of this book is not to try to convince people to do something against their will. However, my contention is that every Sunday School teacher and most of the other workers in the Sunday School are already engaged in some form of counseling.

Some of this counseling takes place in the classroom setting. As the lesson on Gideon was being taught, the teacher, Mary Rice, read Manoah's request of the Lord: "Please, Lord, let the man of God that you sent come back to us and tell us what we must do with the boy when he is born" (Judg. 13:8, GNB). Maria, who was the mother of a teenage daughter who had become quite defiant in recent months, remarked: "I wish I had read that verse fourteen years ago. If I had, maybe we wouldn't be going through the conflict we are at our house right now."

Mary knew that Maria was having some conflicts with her daughter. She responded, "What changes in your relationship with your daughter could you have made that would have changed the way you get along today?"

With that little bit of encouragement, Maria began to pour out the frustration she felt as a parent of a teenager. Other members of the class nodded their heads understandingly, for they had experienced the same thing. The lesson was put aside. The women encouraged and supported Maria and each other. Several shared similar feelings and experiences. When the bell rang for the class to close, Mary asked the eight women present to join hands and to pray for each other and especially for Maria. Then she asked them to agree to pray for Maria during the week.

The teacher of this class had not planned this experience. The lesson writer had not written about it. But a counseling situation had taken place that Sunday morning. Maria had verbalized a need. The class had listened to her and identified with her hurt. This experience did not solve the situation at home. That still remained, but the experience did help change Maria's attitude toward it. The class served as a safety valve for Maria. They had encouraged her. She had been able to verbalize some of her own frustrations. She had heard from the other women that she was not the only one having conflicts with teenagers. All of the women had been encouraged. Counseling had taken place in the classroom that Sunday morning.

Later that week Mary called Maria to see how she was getting along. In the meantime Mary had picked up a copy of a magazine that contained articles about teenagers and how parents and teenagers can work out some of their frustrations. She asked Maria if she could stop by and leave the magazine for her to read.

The problem did not go away. Like so many problems we experience in our daily lives, only time can help the teenager mature so that the constant challenging of the rules is no longer necessary. But Maria found strength in a caring Sunday School class and from a sensitive teacher who took a little time to secure a magazine and make a follow-up visit.

This is a situation the pastor never got involved in. Nor did he necessarily need to be involved. What Maria and her daughter were experiencing was the normal conflict that comes from growing up.

However, this did not mean that they did not need some help in how to deal with the situation. Maria was fortunate in having a sensitive Sunday School teacher who was able to alleviate some of the frustrations she was feeling. The teacher was able to do this because she knew about Maria's situation in advance and was more concerned with meeting needs than in teaching a lesson. That type of encouraging goes on weekly in Sunday School classes all over the nation. With a little guidance the Sunday School class can become a spiritual and emotional DEW line.

This type of ministry does not come automatically. It is something that must be worked at and developed over a long period of time. Sunday School workers must genuinely care for their classes. A worker who does not care will have little or no opportunity to be an encourager. It will be easier to be an encourager if the class is small where you have more personal contact with your class members. A small class will provide an atmosphere for persons to share their needs with a small, caring group. The small Sunday School class becomes a support group in the fullest sense of the word.

Workers must also get to know their members outside of the classroom. It is unlikely that workers will have much ministry as counselors unless they are willing to commit some time to meeting their members on their own territory. This is true at all ages. Children and preschoolers love to have their Sunday School workers visit them in their homes. Adults are not quite as excitable by a visit from a Sunday School worker as children are, but many of them would appreciate a friendly visit and an opportunity to break the routine and loneliness of their lives.

Workers must be willing to become involved in the lives of their members. Ministry takes time, energy, and effort. It is also risky. When one deals with problems in peoples' lives, the risk is always present that the worker will experience some of the problem as well. No worker could minister to a child who is dying of leukemia without becoming personally involved emotionally with the child and his or her family. No one can be close to a person who is involved in a divorce without hurting, too. At many points the worker-counselor may be able to do nothing but to weep with those who are hurting, but few actions bond people together like weeping.

Many positive results come from a ministry of encouragement and counseling. No amount of money can buy the sense of satisfaction that comes when someone squeezes your hand and says, "Thanks for caring. You have helped restore my faith in people and in God."

These benefits, as intangible as they may be, are what inspire Sunday School workers to be encouragers. They will keep us going when we see little progress or even experience failure. Few of us will have the opportunity to encourage people who will perform a task as great as writing three fourths of the New Testament. Yet, to think that our lives have encouraged even one person to pass through successfully the Slough of Despond, as Bunyan called it in his *The Pilgrim's Progress*, will make it all worthwhile.

Notes
1. U. S. Department of Commerce, *Statistical Abstracts of the United States*, Washington, D.C., 1981, p. 60.
2. "Fact Sheet: Estimated Patterns of American Adult Drinking Practices," National Clearinghouse for Alcohol Information, P. O. Box 2345, Rockville, Maryland 20852.
3. *USA Today*, 7 Aug. 1984, p. 1D.

2
Counseling as a Form of Ministry

One of the tasks of a Sunday School class is to minister to its members and potential members. A couple may baby-sit with another couple's children to allow them an opportunity to get away for a few hours. A children's class may make cards to send to one of its members who is sick at home. A class of senior adults may call members daily who live alone to break the monotony of loneliness and to be certain they are all right. A youth class may visit one of its members in the hospital.

Counseling is a form of ministry, also. It is a ministry as much as any of the other forms. Yet, Sunday School workers tend to overlook it as a way of demonstrating concern for people. However, counseling is a way of discovering and meeting physical, emotional, and spiritual needs of class members. It can be the forerunner as well as the follow-up of many other forms of ministry as well.

Bob Siever sat rather quietly in the Sunday School class that morning as the teacher taught a lesson about stewardship of money and the need to support the church's new budget that year. Almost without warning, Bob verbally exploded. He began to accuse the church of being interested only in money and not in people. He criticized the pastor and some recent expenditures the church had made. This caught everyone off guard. It was so unlike Bob. The teacher did not know what to say, so he let Bob talk for a while without trying to respond to his accusations. Bob finally quieted down, and the teacher went on with the lesson. Hoyte Johnson, Bob's group leader for the Sunday School class, made a mental note to check with Bob during the week.

On Tuesday evening Hoyte dropped by to see Bob. Bob had just finished mowing the yard when Hoyte pulled into the drive. After they had talked for a while, Bob said, "Hoyte, I really feel I need to apologize for my outburst Sunday morning, but the lesson just got to me. I really didn't mean all those things I said, but I can't give anything right now. Last Friday I was laid off work at the plant, and I don't know when I'll get to go back. Right now it bothers me that the church wants me to give money when I'm concerned about feeding my family."

Hoyte listened to Bob talk for a while and then told Bob that he had heard about another factory in town that was hiring and suggested Bob apply there.

A week later Bob called Hoyte to tell him he had applied and gotten the job. It didn't pay as much to start with, but the prospects of advancement were good. Bob thanked Hoyte for his help. Then he added, "Thanks for listening to me. I was feeling sorry for myself last Tuesday evening when you came by. Your visit helped."

A counseling session had taken place in the driveway of the Siever's home. Ministry had occurred because a Sunday School worker had cared and sought to encourage a discouraged member in a visible and concrete way. Had Hoyte not dropped by, Bob may have been too embarrassed to have come back to class.

The counseling ministry of the Sunday School worker may involve a number of subjects and take place in a multitude of places. Possibly some explanation is in order as to what the counseling ministry of the Sunday School worker is *not* intended to be.

Counseling by Sunday School workers as viewed in this book is not intended to be done in any formal sense. The author has no desire to make amateur psychologists out of Sunday School workers. In no way will this book suggest that a Sunday School worker establish an office and see patients on a regular basis. The worker-counselor is to be an encourager, a first line of defense that may help take care of a problem before it develops into something more serious.

Some workers may have the ability to do formal counseling, but that type of specialized ministry lies beyond the scope and concern of this book. If workers are interested in the more formal aspects of counseling, they should seek more formal training and supervision. Many states or communities require certification or licensing before a person can engage in formal counseling. Anyone interested in this aspect is encouraged to follow through on the study required. Dedicated Christian counselors are needed, but of all people, Christians should be the best qualified because of their preparation.

In most cases serious problems requiring long-term counseling should be referred to a more qualified counselor than the average Sunday School worker. Irreparable damage can be done by would-be counselors who do not know what they are doing. When worker-counselors encounter persons who need help beyond what they can offer, the person in need should be referred to a pastor or someone with more experience in counseling. A later chapter will deal with how to refer people to the proper place and person without making them feel they have been deserted.

However, Sunday School workers have enough counseling ministry to keep them busy with those aspects they have the skill to handle. One way to help keep things in perspective is to consider the role of the Sunday School worker-counselor as a *first line of defense.*

We lived once in Northern Kentucky. Several small communities in the area carried the name "Fort." These communities formed a semicircle around the Kentucky city of Covington and Cincinnati, Ohio, just across the Ohio River. After several years of wondering, I discovered that these cities originally had been forts built during the Civil War to keep John Hunt Morgan and his raiders from attacking Covington and Cincinnati.

Sunday School workers are like this first line of defense. They will make the first contact, but they will need additional help in case of a real frontal attack. Sunday School workers can rest assured in knowing that many resources beyond their abilities are available to them to provide help in time of need.

This is not to say that Sunday School worker-counselors will never encounter people who have serious problems. They will meet many who have great difficulties. When they do, the wise Sunday School worker-counselor will call in additional help.

Possibly a correct analogy would be a M.A.S.H. unit—a Mobile Army Surgical Hospital—near the front lines. Hospital conditions are far from ideal, but in many cases the wounded need only minor help. Immediate treatment can be given, and the soldiers can return to combat. However, in more serious cases the wounded must be treated immediately to prevent a more serious situation from developing. If the wounded had to be transported a great distance without some medical aid, they would die. But the M.A.S.H. unit can provide emergency help and then send the severely wounded to more expert help and more ideal conditions behind the lines.

This should be the way worker-counselors view their ministry. Many situations can be taken care of quickly. Other situations require more expert skill and time for healing than worker-counselors have. These people need to be referred.

Areas of Need

What are some of the areas of need in which the Sunday School worker-counselor will function? The situations are nearly as numerous as the people one meets. However, some common problems exist in all of our lives. Regardless of where one lives, these problems will be encountered.

Dr. Thomas H. Holmes, a psychiatrist and his colleagues at the University of Washington School of Medicine, developed a "life-events scale" to help measure stress and to alert people to possible dangers. The scale lists forty-three events ranging from death and divorce at one end to going through Christmas and experiencing a minor violation of the law at the other end. Any one of the forty-three situations would be an opportunity for counseling. Look over the list and see how much weight is given to each item.

One word of caution needs to be added. Holmes's studies indicated that persons accumulating more than 200 points in a single year *may* experience more stress than they can stand, and as a result they *may* experience illness.

The key word here is *may*. Some people are able to handle stress better than others. When I moved to my present position, I changed vocations, bought a new home, experienced the death of one of my closest friends, and encountered several other "life events" that appear on the scale. My total for the year was well over 400 points. I readily admit that it was a stressful time, but I did not experience either physical or mental illness.

However, to be aware of the danger level is important. The scale of impact may differ from person to person. Buying a new home and assuming a mortgage over $10,000 (31 points) caused me little or no stress. However, a minor traffic accident (11 points) that was my fault which occurred in front of the church where I was serving as pastor caused me a great deal of stress. (In fact, writing about it nearly six years later still causes me some anxiety!) What causes one person stress because of one's background may not affect another person in the same way. Be cautious about making hard and fast assumptions.

The scale serves as a general guide to stress. Each of these areas listed will create some degree of stress. Although the stress created will differ from person to person, the worker-counselor should be alerted to a possible need for counseling when any of them occur— especially if several of them come simultaneously.

How Different Events Cause Stress[1]

	LIFE EVENT	MEAN VALUE
1.	Death of spouse	100
2.	Divorce	73
3.	Marital separation	65
4.	Jail term	63
5.	Death of close family member	63
6.	Personal injury or illness	53
7.	Marriage	50
8.	Fired at work	47
9.	Marital reconciliation	45
10.	Retirement	45
11.	Change in health of family member	44
12.	Pregnancy	40
13.	Sex difficulties	39
14.	Gain of new family member	39
15.	Business readjustment	39
16.	Change in financial state	38
17.	Death of close friend	37
18.	Change to different line of work	36
19.	Change in number of arguments with spouse	35
20.	Mortgage or loan for major purchase (home, etc.)	31
21.	Foreclosure of mortgage or loan	30
22.	Change in responsibilities at work	29
23.	Son or daughter leaving home	29
24.	Trouble with in-laws	29
25.	Outstanding personal achievement	28
26.	Wife begin or stop work	26
27.	Begin or end school	26
28.	Change in living conditions	25
29.	Revision of personal habits	24
30.	Trouble with boss	23

31.	Change in work hours or conditions	20
32.	Change in residence	20
33.	Change in schools	20
34.	Change in recreation	19
35.	Change in church activities	19
36.	Change in social activities	18
37.	Mortgage or loan for lesser purchase (car, TV, etc.)	17
38.	Change in sleeping habits	16
39.	Change in number of family get-togethers	15
40.	Change in eating habits	15
41.	Vacation	13
42.	Christmas	12
43.	Minor violations of the law	11

When worker-counselors know a Sunday School member is experiencing a time of stress, what can they do? If the worker-counselor is a teacher, one might decide to deal with the particular problem in a general way in the classroom if that is possible.

Mrs. Ramerez knew that Bethany's grandmother had died, and Bethany was having some difficulty in talking about it. During a lesson in the Children's Department that Sunday morning on the death of Lazarus, Mrs. Ramerez asked the boys and girls how they would have felt if Lazarus had been their friend. Then she asked them to draw a picture that would describe how they would have felt. As the boys and girls worked on their pictures, Mrs. Ramerez stopped and talked with Bethany, and Bethany began to describe how she would have felt if she had been Mary or Martha. The picture she drew was of a dog that was growling and showing his teeth. Mrs. Ramerez tried to acknowledge Bethany's anger and to explain that it was all right to feel that way when someone we love dies.

Another way worker-counselors can respond is by going by the house for a visit. If the worker-counselor has a good enough relationship with the member, the matter could be approached directly. If this is not possible, the conversation can be steered in that direction, giving the member an opportunity to express himself at this point. If he does not choose to do so, it may be that he is not ready to accept the matter or has chosen not to talk about it at this time.

A third option may be to write a letter stating that you are aware of the problem and that you respect the member's right to privacy, but at the same time you do not want to deny her the opportunity of a listening ear. Suggest that you would be available to help in any way possible if you are needed. Include your phone number and an expression of your prayer support. The rest is up to the member.

Betty had been absent from Sunday School for several weeks. Word had come to Maria White, her Sunday School teacher, that Betty and her husband had separated and were in the process of getting a divorce. Because she did not want to intrude on Betty's privacy, Maria wrote a short note, expressing her concern for Betty and suggested that they might have lunch some day if Betty wanted to talk. Betty called soon after she received the note and thanked Maria for the offer. She declined to have lunch with her but said that Maria was the only person from the church who had communicated with her in any way. No one else seemed to want to have anything to do with her. Maria assured Betty of her prayer support and told Betty that the offer was still open at anytime in the future if Betty should need a listening ear.

If several people are experiencing the same or related problems, it would be possible to invite someone to speak to the whole class.

Dorothy Newman had taught senior high students for several years. As final exam time approached, she asked the youth director to come speak to the group about cheating. Without condemning the group, the youth director began to lay out some biblical principles and some practical reasons for not cheating. Gradually the group began to open up and to share why they felt it necessary to cheat on exams. The youth director continued to offer sound reasons why cheating was wrong for a Christian. All of the senior highs left with a deeper understanding of what the gospel demands from them in this particular area.

All of these worker-counselors dealt with a problem that could cause stress. Each dealt with it in a different manner. The important point is that they did seek to deal with it. They served as encouragers to the people to whom they ministered.

Where Does One Counsel?

Where does the encourager offer counsel? It can be nearly any-place. The Bible study had been on the Sermon on the Mount that morning. As Janice Bell came out of the worship service into the parking lot, she noticed Natalie Ross, a thirteen-year-old who had been in her Sunday School class that morning. Janice smiled and spoke to Natalie. As she did, Natalie began to sob. Janice put her arm around Natalie and walked out to her car; she suggested that Natalie sit down in the car and talk. Soon a sordid story began to tumble out. Natalie's parents were getting a divorce, and Natalie was caught in the middle between her parents. Her parents had fought most of the night. Her father had left, and her mother had gone on a rampage, beating Natalie's younger sister until Natalie grabbed her sister and locked her sister in her room. Her mother had spent the rest of the night drinking herself into a stupor. Natalie had gotten up that morning and had walked to church. What should she do? She was afraid to go home, yet she feared for her younger sister.

Janice listened to the story and then suggested that Natalie should talk with the pastor, Dr. Howard. She offered to go with her. They walked back into the church and met Dr. Howard as he was coming out of his office. Janice explained the situation and asked Dr. Howard if he could help. He agreed to do what he could, and he and Natalie went into his office. Janice went on her way, praying for Natalie and her family.

In this situation, a church parking lot became a place of counseling. Counseling can take place in the classroom, in the hallway after class, or over the phone. It can take place in the counselee's home, in a restaurant, at a social activity, during a chance meeting in a shopping center. In short, the counselor-teacher can use nearly anyplace and anytime to practice the ministry of encouragement. Because of the inappropriateness of some places, the worker-counselor may suggest a quieter place and a more convenient time.

This kind of "meanwhile ministry" was the same kind that Jesus practiced. Again and again, He met someone while He was on His way to another appointment. He encountered Zacchaeus (Luke 19:1-9) and blind Bartimaeus (Mark 10:46-52) on the way to Jerusalem to die. He counseled the Samaritan woman (John 4:1-42) on His way to Galilee. He provided healing for the woman who had suffered from severe bleeding for twelve years (Luke 8:40-48) while He was on His way to heal Jairus's daughter. As one studies the life of Jesus, the overwhelming conclusion is that most of what Jesus did could be termed a "meanwhile ministry." So much of what He did was while He was in the midst of doing another task.

The counseling-encouraging ministry of the Sunday School worker will be much like that. Few Sunday School workers will deliberately set out to establish a counseling ministry. However, they can be alert to the many opportunities they have to meet people's needs in a "meanwhile ministry." They have the finest example in the world after whom to pattern their ministry—Jesus Christ.

How to Create a Climate for Counseling

How do worker-counselors create a climate for counseling? How can they get class members to trust them enough to share their needs with them?

Would-be counselors cannot enlist counselees just by telling people that they are available. More is required than that, although that may be a beginning. Worker-counselors must demonstrate a compassion for people. A statement that they care will fall on deaf ears unless the workers have demonstrated genuine compassion and understanding previously.

Another opening worker-counselors can use is to let people know that they have some needs in their own lives. People relate to weakness much easier than they relate to strength. Teachers who can share some of their own struggles during their teaching will encourage class members to approach them. Those workers who do not teach can demonstrate an openness in the class discussions that will communicate that they know what it means to hurt and to experience failure in their lives. Preschool and children's workers can demonstrate a spirit of openness as they teach and as they visit with parents of the children they teach.

A person who has experienced a problem with temptation in a particular area will be able to relate better to a teacher who admits to being tempted. That is why the Bible tells us Jesus was tempted but did not sin (Heb. 4:15). We relate easier to one who knows something about our problems. Teachers who refuse to admit to any problems will not encourage people to share their problems with them. They will tend to turn people away.

Think about your own situation. If you had a particular need, would you feel more inclined to ask for help from someone you knew who had experienced that same need or someone you felt had never been involved with that problem? Most of us would prefer to talk with someone who had experienced the same problem we are wrestling with because we would feel that person would come nearer understanding just how we feel and what we can do to solve the problem.

This is not to say that persons who have not shared their problems do not have any problems. That certainly is a false assumption. Some persons may have more problems in that area than one who shares, but the only way we know about their problems is for them to share with us. Sharing with others encourages them to share with us.

However, teachers must be careful not to let the class sessions become a confessional. They must use discretion in what, how, and when they share. However they do it, those who are willing to take the risk will open up opportunities to counsel those who are in their class.

One word of warning needs to be injected here. Not everyone will respond favorably to this approach. Some people are uncomfortable with knowing that their spiritual leaders are not perfect. I shared once in a sermon that I was not comfortable in sharing my faith in a personal encounter. This upset one woman in the congregation because her pastor was not able to measure up in an area where she felt he should excel. Later, I was able to get some training in personal evangelism and was better able to share my faith in personal encounters. I wanted to share this with this woman, but she could not hear me because of my previous statement.

However, enough others responded favorably to my sharing that I felt the risk was worth taking. By sharing my feelings of inadequacy, others were able to express their need and begin to work toward overcoming it.

Worker-counselors who make themselves vulnerable do run a risk. Yet it is one that is worth taking. It is the most effective way to make oneself available for a counseling-encouraging ministry.

Counseling is indeed a form of ministry that every Sunday School worker can practice. It is one that requires time, energy, and effort. Yet, it is one that can bring special rewards to all who are willing to make the effort and take the risk.

Note

1. Reprinted with permission from *Journal of Psychosomatic Research,* vol. 11, T. H. Holmes and R. H. Rahe, "The Social Readjustment Rating Scale," Copyright 1967, Pergamon Press, Ltd.

3
Suggestions for Counseling
(Part 1)

How do worker-counselors go about counseling? The kind of counseling Sunday School workers will do will be practical and down to earth. It will not be formal counseling in the sense that a professional counselor would practice. This chapter and the next will discuss twelve suggestions to help worker-counselors in their ministry of encouragement. These are not hard-and-fast rules—at least not in most cases.

Listen! Listen! Listen!

The first suggestion is to listen! listen! listen! I thought about making this all twelve suggestions. It is unlikely that the worker-counselor will find any suggestion more helpful than this one.

Our society is impersonal. To the government I am a number; to my bank I am another number. My name is relatively unimportant to any business. My account number that will match their computer is more important than my name. Few people talk. Fewer still listen.

I once met a friend I had not seen for sometime. I had several things I wanted to tell her. However, I could not get a word in edgewise. She talked constantly. I finally resigned myself to listening to her. I later concluded that she needed someone to listen to her more than I needed someone to listen to me.

A story made the rounds sometime back about two doctors who met in a hospital corridor. One doctor remarked to the other, a psychiatrist: "I don't know how you can spend all your day listening to people." The psychiatrist replied, "So, who listens?"[1]

Who does listen? Certainly a Sunday School worker who wants to help people will listen. However, listening is not easy. It can be difficult. It is not necessarily something that comes naturally. The following suggestions can help you become a good listener.

Look at the Speaker

To say that one must look at the speaker to be a good listener seems almost unnecessary. Yet, all of the rest of these suggestions will seem just as unnecessary to someone who listens. However, stop and think of some recent conversations you have had. Did you get the impression that the person was not listening to you? Instead of looking at you, was the person looking at the clock, out of the window, or at a host of other things? Most of us have had that experience. The other side of the coin is that most of us have done that when we were supposedly listening to someone. We were listening with only about half of our interest. With the other half we were checking the time, thinking of things we had to do, making mental notes to do an errand as soon as this conversation ended, or thinking about what we were going to say as soon as we got our chance. We have all done that. That is why persons who are speaking to us know instinctively that we are not listening fully when we do not look at them. They have played that same game and are wise to us.

Pay Attention

Give the speaker your undivided attention. It is possible to look intently at the speaker and let your mind be elsewhere. Again, speakers are aware of this tactic because they have done it too. Regardless of how busy you are, it will take no more time to give the speaker your full attention than it will to give only partial. In fact, it may require less time. You may be able to understand the situation quicker and get to the point in less time.

Resist the Urge to Tell a Similar Story

Resist the urge to tell a similar story or experience of your own. Beth's husband had just died. Anne came to see her at her home. As Beth talked about her grief, Anne replied, "I know just how you feel. My husband died two years ago. I can't tell you how difficult it is. It is especially hard at night when I get ready to go to bed. In fact, I usually stay up late at night until I am dead tired before I even go into the bedroom." On and on she went talking about her own grief.

Beth sat and listened for a while, then she let her mind trail off to some other thoughts.

Anne's grief was real. Her attempt at identifying with Beth's grief may have been legitimate, but the way she did it was inappropriate. Beth did not need to hear about Anne's grief at that point. She needed someone to listen to her. What real value does identification serve? Does it really help me to know that you have experienced the same grief as I have? I think not. When I am hurting, I am not interested in you. I am concerned with my own hurt. I am selfish and self-centered. I am concerned only about myself.

Ask Leading Questions

Another way to be a good listener is to ask leading questions. To ask pertinent questions demonstrates that you are giving the speaker your full attention. Your questions draw the speaker out.

Leading questions should not give the appearance of prying. That is not the purpose of questions. Questions should encourage and open the door for speakers to go through if they so desire.

Leading questions are not answerable by one-word responses. The following exchange took place between a teacher and a class member:

MEMBER: I get very angry when I think about all the little children who die each year.

TEACHER: Are you angry at God?

MEMBER: No.

This teacher, instead of asking a leading question that would encourage the class member to share deeper feelings, asked a question that brought an abrupt end to a particular line of pursuit. A more appropriate approach would have been the following:

MEMBER: I get very angry when I think about all the little children who die each year.

TEACHER: Do you feel God could have prevented these deaths?

MEMBER: Well, I had never thought of it that way before, but I guess I do. It makes me angry that He doesn't stop this kind of thing if He is able to do it.

This kind of questioning provided an opportunity for the person to verbalize a feeling. Few people will admit being angry at God. However, given an opportunity to express their feelings of anger they would do that. By asking leading questions the worker-counselor can provide opportunities for people to voice some of their deeper feelings.

Be Interested

A final suggestion for a good listener is to be interested in what the speaker says. Admittedly, this may be hard at times. Often we may want to say with the psychiatrist, "So, who listens?" If you are not interested in what the person is talking about, you will not be a good listener. The speaker will soon understand that you are not listening, and you will cut yourself off from the person. Many opportunities present themselves for us to apply the Golden Rule, but surely this is one of them. What I say is important to me. If you will listen to me, I like you. If you do not, I will try to find someone who will listen. If you would like people to be interested in what you are saying, then you should listen to them.

Never Divulge Confidences

I am tempted to begin each of these suggestions by saying that this is the most important of them all. It may be that all of the suggestions are equally important, but if so, this suggestion is certainly a first among equals!

Divulging confidences carries the potential of hurting people deeply. How tragic it is to share with someone something that you intended for that person alone and then to discover that it was broadcast to the world.

Sherrie H. was twenty-six years old. Her husband, Mike, was an attorney. He had just finished law school and gotten settled in his new position. In order to get ahead, Mike spent many evenings working at the office or at home. Sherrie, because they had few friends, enrolled in a pottery class one evening a week. This gave her something to do.

The first evening she met Bill. Bill was just a little older than she was and, as she found out later, had just gone through a divorce. Bill was a very sensitive person. As they worked, they talked. Sherrie found that she began to look forward to these sessions because Bill listened to her and seemed to care about her—something Mike did little of in recent weeks.

One evening after class, several of the pottery class, including Bill and Sherrie, stopped and got a cup of coffee. This became a weekly ritual. However, the rest of the group soon dropped out, and Bill and Sherrie were stopping each evening after class by themselves. Then one night when Mike was working, Sherrie met Bill for dinner. Gradually, without her intending it to happen, she became quite involved with Bill.

Sherrie had been brought up in a Christian home, and she and Mike were members of a church. One evening when Mike was working, Mike and Sherrie's Sunday School teacher dropped by for a visit. During the course of the visit, Sherrie's guilt over her relationship with Bill caused her to "confess" to her teacher what was going on in her life.

At the next meeting of the workers and teachers in the Sunday School Department, the teacher, under the guise of sharing a "prayer" request, shared Sherrie's story with all of the group. Soon word got back to Sherrie about what had happened. Needless to say she was angry, embarrassed, and lived in constant fear that Mike would find out, too. She stopped going to church and retreated from most of her social contacts.

That which is told in confidence must never be revealed. It may be hard to keep a juicy bit of information, but we should stop and consider the damage that can be done to a person or persons involved.

Somewhere I read of a young girl who happened to be playing outside an open window. Inside the house, her mother and neighbor were talking. The neighbor shared some personal problems with the woman, and the young girl accidentally overheard what she said. Later when her mother discovered that her daughter had overheard the conversation, she cautioned the girl about revealing what she had heard. Then she said, "If Mrs. _____ had left her purse or some other valuable here, you would not have stolen it. Neither must you take what you have heard. You must leave it right here."

The following suggestions might help you to keep confidences.

Make a Covenant with Your Tongue

Job, in defense of his integrity, declared: "I made a covenant with mine eyes; why then should I think upon a maid?" (Job 31:1). This is good advice in sexual matters, but it can also be good advice in other areas as well. Sunday School worker-counselors can say: "I have made a covenant with my tongue; why then should I reveal a confidence?"

Keeping confidences begins long before people confide in you. You must decide in advance that you will never knowingly reveal something that someone has shared with you. Decide in advance that you will make a covenant with your tongue to remain silent about what those who have trusted you have shared with you.

Don't Seek Popularity at Others' Expense

All of us want to be liked and be popular. We feel special when someone shares a secret with us because that makes us feel that the person likes us. Sharing secrets is also a way to try to get people to like us. If we share secrets with people, we think they will like us more.

The popularity and praise of others is never worth the sacrifice it costs to violate a confidence. Worker-counselors must be so assured of their identity that they will not give in to the temptation to divulge something that ought not pass their lips. When you are tempted to disclose even something that may not be too damaging, remember Sherrie and the destruction a violated confidence caused in her life.

Saint Francis of Assisi once had a woman come to him and confess that she had been gossiping about her neighbors. She was truly sorry for what she had done and asked for God's forgiveness for her sin. Francis readily assured her of God's forgiveness. Then the woman asked what she could do to make amends for her sin. Francis instructed her to place a feather on the doorstep of each home where someone lived about whom she had lied. The woman soon returned and said she had done what he had commanded. Then Francis instructed her to retrace her steps and gather the feathers and return them to him.

In a short time the woman returned in tears saying that the wind had scattered the feathers, and she could not possibly retrieve them. Then Frances gently told her that although God would forgive her for her sin, she could never undo all the damage she had done with her words.

Irreparable damage can be done by revealing those confidences shared with you. This damage is done not only to the counselee, but it can also damage *you*, the worker-counselor. To know that you have violated a confidence can cause grief and pain far beyond the fleeting pleasure you might derive from sharing some tidbit of gossip.

Assure Counselees of Confidentiality

You may need to assure those whom you encourage that what they share with you will be kept in strictest confidence. You can do this in the classroom in at least two ways. You can say it. You can share with your class that you have "made a covenant with your tongue" and are able to keep confidences. More important than saying it, you can demonstrate it. Be certain that you do not give even the slightest impression that you are using material someone has shared with you as an illustration in the Sunday School lesson.

Mrs. Shields had caught Josh stealing some money from the Sunday School offering basket. She had warned him not to do it again and explained to him that it was wrong. Josh had promised he would never do it again if she would not tell anyone.

One Sunday the children were studying the Ten Commandments. Mrs. Shields took this opportunity to warn all the children that stealing was wrong. She specifically singled out stealing from the offering basket. Although she did not mention Josh's name, Josh felt everyone knew what he had done. He was embarrassed and angry and felt betrayed. The next Sunday morning he had a "stomach ache" and did not feel like going to Sunday School. The following Sunday it was the same thing. Soon his parents could not get him to go at all.

Josh grew to manhood hating church. He knew that what he had done was wrong, but he felt that Mrs. Shields had taken unfair advantage of him. It was only as an adult that he was able to accept that Mrs. Shields was not perfect either, and he could forgive her and himself for what had happened.

Identify Those Involved in the Confidence

One caution needs to be offered about confidentiality. Often people will share something with you and ask you to keep it confidential. Assure them that you will do that but then ask how many other people know what they have told you. If others know about the situation, you can assure the people that you will not reveal what they have told you, but you cannot control what others will do. This way you protect yourself and your integrity from being questioned about something you did not do.

Having said all of this, there may be a time that you will have to violate a confidence. Be absolutely certain, however, that it is necessary and that the value of violating a confidence is greater than the damage done.

If you suspect that someone needs more professional help than you can give, ask the person for permission to share that need with your pastor or other counselor. (See chapter 7 for more information on referral.) If the person refuses, and in your estimation he or she needs medical or psychiatric help, you may need to share that need with others. If, for example, the person is threatening suicide or is threatening to inflict bodily harm on others, this would justify your violating a confidence. If you are aware of a situation involving child abuse, you are required by law to report it to the authorities. You are assured of anonymity. The child welfare agency in your area will investigate the situation.

Violating confidence is so potentially explosive that you must be certain that it is worth the risk.

Give Advice Cautiously

All of us are flattered when someone comes to us and asks us for advice. It is somewhat reassuring that at last someone has recognized that we have great stores of knowledge and wisdom and can advise and instruct.

However, in most cases we should avoid giving advice like we would avoid the plague! But what about all those poor, miserable people in the world who don't know what direction to go?

True, some people do not know what decisions to make, but two inherent risks exist in our telling them.

The first risk is that we may be wrong in our advice. We may not have all of the facts of a given situation. Without all the facts, we may come up with wrong answers. Even with all the facts, because we are fallible, we may make a mistake.

The second risk is that even if we are right in our advice, we rob the persons from making the decision. We make the decision instead of letting them do it. Often these people are the ones who need most to make their own decisions and to stand on their own feet. When we give advice, we make people dependent on us. This may stroke our ego, but it does not help the people.

Instead of giving advice, help people discover the alternatives for themselves. From your perspective you may be able to see several alternatives. Surely the person you are counseling has some ideas. In fact, most of the time, unless the person is mentally ill, the person knows what course of action to take and just needs someone to bounce his alternatives off of. It is not unusual to listen for some time, asking leading questions, and then to have the person thank you for your advice when you really haven't given any! But that's the way it ought to be. Decisions people have arrived at themselves will be more lasting if these are their decisions rather than coming from someone else.

Be Cautious Where You Counsel

The young married couples' department had gone to a state park for a weekend retreat. It was a deeply spiritual experience for all involved. Janice Evans, who had been brought in to lead the retreat on how couples could enrich their marriages, had done a masterful job. Saturday night after the session, Joe Birch asked to talk with her about some of the things she had said. Because several people were still in the lounge, Janice invited Joe to her room where they could have some privacy. They talked for about an hour, and then Joe left. However, as he left, he happened to meet some of the group just as he walked out of Janice's room. He really didn't think too much about it until a few days later when he learned that a vicious rumor was being circulated about him and "that conference leader."

Worker-counselors cannot be too cautious about where they counsel. The biblical admonition to "abstain from all appearance of evil" (1 Thess. 5:22) is good advice.

Human nature being what it is, such situations as the one described between Janice and Joe can be dangerous. A close connection exists between heightened spiritual insight and heightened sexual desire. John Bunyan's *The Pilgrim's Progress* ends with the insight that "there was a way to hell even from the gates of heaven."[2] More than one religious worker can testify to the correctness of Bunyan's insight. Satan is ever alert to the times we are at our weakest. Wise worker-counselors will be cautious where they counsel.

Other reasons for exercising caution have nothing to do with sexual indiscretion or innuendo. A class member who, in the midst of a class session, begins to share intimate details about an illegal activity he and others are involved in may regret later having "dumped" before the whole class. A wise teacher would suggest that they get together at a more convenient time when they could talk in privacy.

Crowded restaurants, shopping malls, or halls at church are not appropriate places for sharing intimate details about personal experiences. Too much possibility exists for someone to overhear what is being said. That could cause embarrassment for the person and allow that person to accuse you of having violated a confidence.

This does not mean that worker-counselors must have a private office. However, under some circumstances, you may want to borrow the pastor's office or another office at church. The privacy of a home or a restaurant where you can talk without interruption may work in other situations. Be cautious where you counsel.

Be Alert to Warning Signals

Some people predict a change in weather because of an ache in a big toe. Meteorologists make their predictions based on sophisticated computer information. Both may be right sometimes, and both may be wrong. However, most of us would more likely trust the meteorologists for our weather predictions because they know how better to read the signs.

Worker-counselors will also be alert to some of the warning signs in the lives of their class members. The more familiarity we have with these signs, the more likely it is that we will pick up on a critical situation. This doesn't mean that we will always be right. Nor does it mean that when these signs occur that they are always an indication of some serious problem. A general guideline is that *when any radical change in behavior occurs, be alert to the possibility of some deeper problem.*

Juanita Moore was forty-three years old. She was married and the mother of two children, the last of whom had just left for college. Juanita had always been fairly active in church work but had never taken an active part in the visitation program of the Sunday School. She came to her Sunday School teacher, Mary Alice Ware, and told her that she wanted to start visiting. So Mary Alice gave her a list of the inactive members and prospects for the class.

One day the teacher received a call from the pastor asking about Juanita. She had visited a prospective family and had told them that they were going to hell unless they started coming to church. The pastor asked the teacher to visit Juanita and see what was going on since this was rather unusual behavior for her.

Mary Alice called Juanita and went by to see her. As the two women talked, Juanita began to describe a vision she had had.

She said the Lord had appeared to her and told her that she was His special messenger to prepare the world for His return. She was to warn everyone. This message was so urgent that she did not even have time to eat and sleep.

As Mary Alice looked around she could see that little time had been spent in cleaning the house. Dirty dishes with dried food were stacked in the sink and still on the table. This was such a change from Juanita's usual behavior. She had always been an immaculate housekeeper. She had not worked outside her home, and she had given herself to making her home a beautiful showplace.

After talking with Juanita for a while, Mary Alice left and went by to see the pastor. She shared with him what she had found, and the pastor called her husband to discuss the matter with him. Juanita's husband confirmed that they had been having some problems in recent months, and since their last child had gone to college things had gotten worse.

Juanita's husband took her to the doctor. She was not hospitalized, but it was necessary for her to receive medication and to have several months of professional counseling.

Taken at one level, some of Juanita's behavior was certainly not out of the ordinary. Many people are fervent visitors for their church, and many people leave dirty dishes in the sink. However, such a drastic change all at once in so many different areas was an indication that something was going on. The guideline: *when any radical change in behavior occurs, be alert to the possibility of some deeper problem.*

Changes seem to show up first in several areas. Drastic changes in eating, sleeping, elimination, or any other physical change can be warning signals. Juanita was not eating nor sleeping. Her normally spotless house was a shambles. Other warning signals could be a change in spending habits. If one has always been a generous person and suddenly becomes excessively selfish and stingy, or if one has always been conservative financially and begins to spend money and make excessive charges, these can be warning signals.

A change in a person's moral code can also be a warning of deeper problems. A person who would never steal anything who begins to shoplift, or a person whose sexual code suddenly changes, may be experiencing some emotional problems.

These changes in a person's behavior are not absolute proofs of mental illness; they are warning signs that something *may* be wrong. Worker-counselors will take these as warning signs and look for further indications of problems. This would be a good time for you to talk to your pastor or some other competent counselor to get more experienced advice.

Be Sensitive

So much of an encourager's ministry is based on sensitivity. Sensitivity is almost like a sixth sense that a person has. It is impossible to set up rules and absolutes in dealing with people. All that can be done is to offer guidelines for helping, but beyond that, a worker-counselor must possess a special sensitivity to people's needs.

As in all the areas of our lives, Jesus is our example here, too. Read through the Gospels and note how sensitive He was to the needs of others. When Jesus healed a blind man, He took him away from the crowd where they could have some privacy (Mark 8:24). Jesus wept over Mary and Martha's grief at the death of Lazarus (John 11:35). Jesus refused to look at the woman who had been caught committing adultery (John 8:1-11). He provided wine at the wedding feast in Cana (John 2:1-11) to eliminate embarrassment on the part of the host. Jesus sought to encourage Peter by a special appearance after His resurrection (Luke 24:34), so Peter would be able to forgive himself for having denied Jesus. I would like to think if Judas had stayed around until after the resurrection that Jesus would have appeared to him, too.

This marvelously sensitive Person cares about people's needs. By His sensitivity He is able to determine what we need. He does not treat us all alike, but He tailors His help to our needs.

Encouragers will model their lives after Jesus. They will study His life. They will read the Gospels so they will know about His historical appearance. They will study His relationships with people. They will be so familiar with Jesus' life and teachings that they will know instinctively how Jesus would respond in situations.

This does not mean that they will not be firm or even severe in their actions and words when the situation demands it. On one occasion, Jesus sharply criticized the Pharisees. One of the teachers of the Law took exception to what Jesus had said: "Teacher, when you say this, you insult us too!" (Luke 11:45, GNB). Then Jesus began to criticize the teachers of the law as well. In this circumstance, Jesus knew that this was what was needed most. Sensitivity does not mean cowardice. It means knowing when one should be caustic and when one should be gentle and having the courage to act as the occasion demands.

Notes

1. John Drakeford, *The Awesome Power of the Listening Ear* (Waco: Word Books, 1967), p. 24.

2. John Bunyan, *The Pilgrim's Progress* (New York: Washington Square Press, Inc., 1957), p. 157.

4
Suggestions for Counseling
(Part 2)

People are not machines or robots. They do not always react the same way under the same circumstances. If they did, a neat system of rules could be devised. Counselors could memorize these rules, and, like a mechanic repairing a robot, they could make adjustments in people's lives until they operated properly.

But people are not like that. Each person is an individual. Each person needs special attention. These suggestions are not rules. These suggestions are intended only as guidelines to be mediated through your personality after much prayer and wisdom. They are, however, worthy of your consideration as you seek to perform your ministry of encouragement. Consider them carefully.

Do Not Condemn

A wise encourager will be cautious about condemning people for their sins and failures. This is not to say that what the people we counsel have done is right; it is to say that condemnation is God's responsibility, not ours. When we condemn others, we place ourselves in the position of being God. We set ourselves up as authorities when that is a position reserved for God Himself.

Condemnation is the work of the Holy Spirit. He is the One who judges us for our wrong attitude and actions. We should leave any condemnation to Him rather than to undertake it ourselves.

Condemnation is self-defeating. When we condemn someone for a particular action, our purpose is to bring about a change in behavior. However, it usually has just the opposite effect. If you are married, think back to the last time your spouse criticized you. What was your response? Did you want to change your actions or did you want to continue them in spite? Or what about the last time you were criticized by an employer or someone else? What was your response then? The people we counsel will feel no different than we feel when we are criticized.

In most cases, we know we are guilty already, and we do not need anyone else to tell us. I read somewhere of a prophet of doom standing on the street corner. As people walked by, he would point his finger at them, and declare, "Guilty!" One man, confronted in this manner, remarked to his companion, "Yes, but how did he know?"

We know we are guilty, and especially when we have worked up enough courage to bare our souls to someone and confess our guilt, we do not need someone to condemn us for what we have confessed.

Dan was in the midst of some serious troubles at home. He and Susan had been married for fourteen years. Nothing was really wrong, yet nothing was really right. Susan seemed so tied up in the children and her job that she had no time for him. He felt that all the family was interested in was his paycheck. No one was interested in meeting his needs. Besides that, one of the new female buyers at work had just recently gone through a divorce. They started having lunch together. Then they were both sent out of town together to a product show. They spent the week together, and the last night before they came home, he had spent the night in her room.

Dan justified it by saying that no one would ever know. No one was hurt, and a lot of other people did the same thing.

However, there was just one problem: Dan knew. The experience began to gnaw at him. He couldn't go to church and sit in a Bible study or in a worship service without feeling uncomfortable. He began to invent reasons for not going to church.

He had missed several Sundays when Harold Stivers, one of the men in his Sunday School class, called him and asked to have lunch. They met at a private club where Harold was a member. They sat in the corner of the room where they had some privacy. As they talked, Dan's guilt overcame him. He had always had a great deal of respect for Harold, and Dan felt he could confide in him. Soon the whole story came tumbling out.

As Dan talked he sensed a change in Harold's attitude. Harold's face hardened. His friendliness vanished. When Dan had finished, Harold looked at him coldly and said, "Dan, I'm ashamed of you. You know that adultery is wrong. The Bible says so. You know our church does not approve of your actions. I just can't believe that you would do such a thing." Can you imagine Dan's response?

Actually, Harold did not respond like that. Instead of having a judgmental, critical attitude, Harold let Dan talk. When he had finished Harold asked, "How does this make you feel?" Dan replied, "Terrible! I really do love Susan and the kids. I know the situation at home is not the best, but I also know I would be the same person in a different situation. I don't want a divorce. I want to work at my marriage and make it better. But I don't know how."

Harold affirmed Dan's desire to improve his relationship with Susan and suggested that they pray together. They bowed their heads, and Dan confessed his sin and asked God to forgive him and help him to make his marriage a better one.

As they walked out of the restaurant, Harold suggested that Dan might want to talk with their pastor and get some help in how to put his marriage back together. He assured Dan of his concern and prayer support and that he would keep confidential what Dan had shared with him.

If one does not condemn, what approach is taken? How does one handle a confession? The Bible has a word of advice: "Confess your faults one to another, and pray one for another, that ye may be healed" (Jas. 5:16). Confession is biblical, but as difficult as it may be to confess our sins to someone else, it may be even more difficult to receive the confession. Yet, one of the aspects of the priesthood of the believer is that we act as priests to each other when a need exists.

Assure persons that God will forgive them. A good assurance from the Bible is 1 John 1:9: "If we confess our sins to God, he will keep his promise and do what is right: he will forgive us our sins and purify us from all our wrongdoing" (GNB).

This assurance can be given orally—and probably should. We need to hear this word from God. It helps us to accept it. The person to whom we have confessed does not forgive; he only serves as an agent acting in behalf of God to give God's message to the penitent sinner.

A person also needs to forgive himself. At times, it is hard to believe that we could actually have done what we did. In some circumstances it is easier for me to receive God's forgiveness than it is to forgive myself. My experience leads me to believe that many other people have the same problem. A sensitive worker-counselor will lead a person to see that we must accept God's forgiveness before it is effective.

An encourager who does not condemn a person may have the opportunity of serving as the confessor to a hurting person and seeing God's forgiveness fill that person's life.

Avoid Saying, "I Know How You Feel"

Jan had been at the funeral home all evening receiving friends who had come to express their sorrow at the death of her husband, Bill. Bill had been only fifty-two when he died unexpectedly in his sleep. The line of well-wishers was long. People from all over the community had come to extend their sympathies. Bill had been quite active in civic, church, and political organizations. So many people said so many good things about Bill that Janice almost began to believe them.

Ruth, whose husband had died a few months earlier, came through the line and expressed her sympathy to Jan by saying, "I know just how you feel. I lost my Vernon just eight months ago. I know just how you feel."

To herself Jan thought, "Oh, really? I bet you don't." What few people knew was that Bill was a "Dr. Jekyll and Mr. Hyde." To the world, Bill presented a picture of the perfect gentleman. He was the first to suggest that the church help someone in need.

At home, however, Bill was just the opposite. He was abusive, inconsiderate, and at times even violent. He drank late at night, and on the night of his death he and Jan had had a fight over his drinking and his decision to take some "pills" he had for "headaches." He had become quite violent and had knocked her around until she got out of the room and went into another room and locked the door to keep him away from her. He had then gone back to the living room and had continued his drinking. That's where Jan had found him early the next morning, dead.

Ruth did not know how Jan felt. While Jan was grieved because of Bill's death and the changes it would mean for her, she also felt somewhat relieved that she would not have to put up with Bill's abuse and hypocrisy any longer. *No,* she thought as Ruth moved away from her, *you really do not know how I feel.*

Telling people that you know just how they feel is always dangerous. The truth is that no one knows exactly how anyone else feels about anything. We tell people that we know how they feel in order to identify with them. I am not convinced that this identification is necessary or even desirable. Much of the time we use this expression not so much because we think it will help them but because we do not know what else to say. We are often speechless in the face of grief and death. Grief and death call to mind our own unresolved grief, and we say that which is fresh on our minds. Instead of talking about the other person's grief, it becomes a way of talking about our own. We may be still grieving over our losses of recent years, and we seize upon the opportunity to work on our grief.

If we do not say "I know how you feel!" what do we say? I never feel more inadequate than at the time of death or severe grief. I am a "words" person. I use a lot of words, and I feel that there ought always to be a right word. I have groped for some formula to speak at the time of grief, but I have not found it. I have concluded that at times the best word may be no word. Our presence speaks for us. An embrace, a squeeze of the hand, an assurance that we are praying for the person may be more helpful than trying to speak words that are not true. In the sounds of silence we may communicate and provide more help than in the misuse of words.

Having said this, let me now offer a disclaimer and share an experience. I had served several churches as a student pastor but had little experience in ministering at the time of death. In fact, I had nearly seven years of pastoral experience before I buried a church member. At a funeral I conducted early in my ministry, I learned an important lesson. I was standing in the funeral home trying to offer some comfort to the widow. My theological training was woefully inadequate. As I searched for the right "word," a woman brushed past me, embraced the widow and said, "I know, I know just how you feel."

I have reflected on that experience often over the years. I always felt that that woman did more ministry in that moment than I did with my theological bungling. Her presence counted. I never questioned the widow, but I wonder if the woman's presence rather than her words were not the main source of comfort.

The suggestion at the beginning of this section is: *"Avoid* saying 'I know how you feel.' "* At times you may come close to understanding how someone feels. Be certain, however, that you do know the situation. In most cases, your presence will speak more than your words. If nothing else works, it may be that the best thing you can do is to cry with the person.

Know the Bible's Psychology

An encourager will know the Bible and the way the Bible approaches life. The practice of psychology as we know it today was, of course, unknown in the biblical era. However, that does not mean that the Bible does not contain valid psychological insights. The Bible does, indeed, contain insights into human personality. It should; it was inspired by God who created the human personality.

Worker-counselors who take seriously their counseling and encourager role will immerse themselves in the knowledge and wisdom of the Bible. They will read it, study it, memorize it. They will read books about the Bible, its customs, its language. They will understand the different kinds of literature that the Bible contains. The Bible is our guide for the encouraging ministry. Somehow the idea has emerged that one cannot believe in the Bible and believe in the concept of modern psychology. Nothing could be further from the truth. True psychology and true biblical studies will support and nurture each other. Pseudopsychology and pseudoreligion will always be at odds with each other. That is why it is so imperative that worker-counselors immerse themselves in God's Word.

This does not mean that we memorize a few verses of Scripture and rip them out of context to prove our points. It means that we adopt the spirit of the Bible and learn how to relate to people as the Bible advises.

We can prove anything we want to by the Bible. (Remember the old "Judas went out and hanged himself," "Go thou and do likewise," "Whatsoever thou doest, do quickly" story!) Encouragers should have a special love and reverence for God's Word. They will be the best interpreters of the Scripture because the Scripture is so full of practical, common sense. They will know the precepts of the Bible because these precepts will help them as they work and minister to people.

It would be impossible to list all the psychological insights the Bible contains. That would take many books. However, the following are some of the basic psychological insights that can help worker-counselors.

Forgiveness Is Essential

Forgiveness, whether for ourselves or for others, is essential. The Bible speaks much about the need for forgiveness. Those who refuse to forgive others have no room in their hearts to receive God's forgiveness (Matt. 6:15). A bitter, unforgiving spirit will affect everything else a person does. It can affect our mental, spiritual, and physical health. That is why we are taught to ask for forgiveness for ourselves (Matt. 6:12) and to extend forgiveness to others (Matt. 6:14-15).

At times, it is easier to accept God's forgiveness than it is to forgive ourselves. This unwillingness to forgive ourselves places us in an awkward position. In the fullest sense of the word, our unwillingness to forgive ourselves is idolatry. Only God can forgive or refuse to forgive sin. Therefore, when we refuse to forgive ourselves for something we have done, we place ourselves in the position of God. We make ourselves the highest authority—higher even than God. We make ourselves an idol.

Forgiveness is essential for us all. The Bible is clear that before we can be properly related to God or others, we must both give and receive forgiveness.

The Bible Deals with Basic Issues

The Bible deals with basic issues, not those that appear on the surface. This is a refrain that runs all the way through the Bible, especially the Old Testament. The people offered sacrifices and performed the rituals of worship. They thought that was sufficient. But God declared: "I hate your religious festivals; I cannot stand them! When you bring me burnt offerings and grain offerings, I will not accept them; I will not accept the animals you have fattened to bring me as offerings. Stop your noisy songs; I do not want to listen to your harps. Instead, let justice flow like a stream, and righteousness like a river that never goes dry" (Amos 5:21-25, GNB).

Encouragers must be perceptive enough to see that what may appear to be the outward issue may not be the real issue at all. The experience of Bob Siever (referred to in ch. 2) is an example. Outwardly, Bob attacked the church's appeal for money. In reality, he wasn't opposed to the church's appeal for money; he was frustrated and angry because he could not give because he did not have a job.

The Bible reminds us that we often operate at two levels (or more). We say and do things at one level, but we do them for many different reasons. A woman once asked her pastor to pray for her child who had been injured in an accident. The pastor asked what the woman wanted him to pray for. "Pray that my divorced husband will hear about this and come back!" was her reply.

The Bible Holds Out Hope

The Bible is a Book of hope. The hope that it offers is not short-lived nor ill-founded. It is based on the fact that God is our Creator and knows what we need most. An encourager can speak of hope in the face of what the world would call hopelessness. The God we serve is able to work in everything for good with those who love Him (Rom. 8:28, RSV).

Here is one place that an encourager needs to know the Bible thoroughly. One can trace the different ways God has taken what appeared to be failure from man's perspective and turned it into good. This is not to say that we take evil lightly. It is to say that the God we serve is greater than the forces of evil.

If it were not for a firm belief that God can turn evil into good, I could not face tragedy and grief. If nothing redemptive can come from the tragedies we experience, then what purpose is there in life?

The greatest example of good coming out of evil is the resurrection. What looked for all the world like failure, disappointment, defeat, and death became Easter! The affirmation of the Bible is that if God can do that with His Son, He can do it also in our lives.

Prayer Is Effective

An encourager will also utilize the resource of prayer. The Bible affirms that prayer is a valuable resource. Prayer can be offered in the presence of people or can be be done privately. Prayer helps the one who prays and the one prayed for. As James expressed it: "The effectual fervent prayer of a righteous man availeth much" (5:16).

Encouragers will bathe their ministry in prayer. They will lift up their own inadequacies and the needs of the people they counsel.

Give People the Right to Fail

This may be one of the most difficult suggestions for the worker-counselor. It is difficult to stand by and watch people turn away from a right course or to watch them make the wrong decisions. Yet, our concept of the priesthood of the believer says that this is the right of every person.

Jonathan was twenty-three years old. He had used drugs regularly for several years. He was finishing college and realized that his life was empty and void. He had never worked or had any real goals in life. Occasionally, he had attended a Bible study on campus with his roommate. Jon decided he would go and talk to the leader to see if he had any answers. After the study Jon asked to speak privately with the man who had led the group that evening. Jon explained his predicament, the empty feeling he had, and wanted to know what he could do to fill that empty feeling.

The Bible study leader shared with Jon how he could invite Jesus Christ into his life. Jon readily admitted that this sounded like what he needed. However, he said he could not give up using drugs. The teacher realized that using drugs had become a god in Jon's life. Jon struggled with the decision to accept Christ, but he decided he would rather have his drugs than to take a risk on something else. The Bible study leader sat and sadly watched Jon walk out of the room.

How difficult it is to watch people turn away from that which we know to be truth and joy. The above illustration has been intentionally molded after an experience in the Bible that involved a rich young ruler who came to Jesus to ask Him how to obtain eternal life (Luke 18:18-23). In that case Jesus watched the young man go away. He accepted the man's decision to fail.

Jesus is our example in this area, as in all other areas. He never forced or tried to coerce people. Surely watching people turn away was one of the most difficult tasks Jesus had to do. He, so much more than we, knew the terrible result of refusing the gift of eternal life. He could see the potential for good that the young man had. Yet, He let him go away.

We will not win every battle. We will lose some that seem so senseless. Yet if Jesus could not win every person He encountered, how much less successful will we be?

Just as Jesus, we ought to respect the personhood of those we encounter and allow them the right to fail. God will not force people to accept His way against their will.

Don't Try to Defend God

We do not have to try to defend God. God is quite capable of defending Himself. At times we may encounter someone who is angry with God because God did not perform some particular action. That's all right. God is not threatened by our anger any more than we are threatened by a two-year-old who tells us he hates us. We know the two-year-old doesn't mean it. He will soon get over his hurt and forget his anger.

How much less threatened is God by our anger. We do not have to fear that persons will be condemned by God for their expressions of anger. God knows about it already. Nor should we tell angry persons that they shouldn't feel that way. That will not work either. If God is able to forgive those who crucified His Son (Luke 23:24), surely He will forgive those who do not understand His purpose in the death of a child or a dear friend.

I earlier made reference to the death of one of my closest friends. Ron Lewis was a dear friend as well as a colleague. He had been a layman in our church and served as a volunteer youth director. We started looking for a full-time youth and education minister, and we ended up calling "Louie" as the youth had affectionately dubbed him. Louie was a naturally gifted youth leader. He also had a natural gift of sharing his faith. I had neither of these abilities. Ron and I complemented each other in the areas of pastoral ministry as well as any two staff persons I know. I never had a brother, but Ron was as close as a brother could be. When he was thirty, he was stricken with leukemia. In just a little over two years, he had died.

I was hurt, angry. Why would God take someone who had so many gifts the church needed? Why would He take someone whom I needed? Why? With my head I knew that my grief was for my own loss. Yet, the only way I knew to express my grief was to say that I was angry with God.

In trying to illustrate what I have been saying about encouragers not needing to defend God, I shared this experience in a conference I once led. It was a way I could help work through my own grief and also demonstrate to those present that it was all right to express our anger to God.

The response to my sharing in this particular group was interesting. Three different people immediately responded by trying to defend God. One of them told me I should not feel that way. The other two started quoting passages out of the Bible to me to prove that I was wrong in my feelings. For some reason, neither of these approaches offered me any help.

I still miss Ron. Today, we received a Christmas card from his wife. She expressed that she still misses him, but it was not with the same intensity she had missed him the first Christmas. We both are working through our grief. But having someone tell me I should not feel that way and quoting verses out of the Bible to me to prove it did not help me work through my grief. Nor will it help others. God is not threatened by my grief and anger. It may, indeed, represent a lack of faith on my part, but if that lack of faith is there, I need to be honest in admitting it. That is the only way I can ever work through it and develop a stronger faith.

I will survive. I will work through the grief process. I have other friends and resources who have supported and ministered to me. However, others may not be as fortunate as I. Be sensitive to people's needs. Don't feel you have to defend God. He has stood for a long time on His own.

Let Christ Guide You

Christians are Christ's representatives in the world. They do His work in His name. Encouragers should seek to let Christ guide their words and acts so they can perform His ministry to people who are hurting. What you do and say should be Christ acting and speaking through you. Offer yourself to Him. Make yourself available to be His lips, His hands, His feet.

This sounds so elemental, but I assure you it is not. Many people provide secular help, and these people are essential in our society. However, few people provide help in the name of Jesus Christ. An encourager provides that unique contribution.

If providing that ministry is your purpose, then let Christ reign in your life so that your helping becomes an extension of of His life. As you live with Him, you will become more aware of how He would respond, you will become more sensitive to the needs of people, and you will become aware of how best to respond in certain situations.

Sunday School workers who take seriously the encourager ministry will live with Christ so closely that they will begin to think and act like Jesus as they minister in His name.

Don't Hesitate to Refer

What do worker-counselors do when they encounter situations beyond their ability to handle them? They call in extra help! We do this in all areas of our lives. If we need to move a piece of furniture too heavy for one person to lift, we ask someone to help us. If something goes wrong with the car and we do not know how to fix it, we ask someone to help us.

Sunday School workers who encounter situations beyond their ability to provide help need to call in someone else to assist them. It is imperative that they call in extra help. Serious damage can be done if they try to minister in areas in which they have no ability.

The importance of this act of referring is highlighted by the whole chapter (ch. 7) devoted to this subject. There is nothing wrong with asking for help, and you should do so just as soon as you realize the seriousness of the problem. As in other areas, your first line of referral should be your pastor unless you have good reasons for not doing so.

5
Counseling Children

Children are people, too! If more people knew that, we would have less problems when we get to be adults. Many—if not most—of our problems have their roots in our childhood. How we as adults accept death and grief, disappointments and conflicts, depends in large measure on how we were taught to do this as children.

Children are so refreshing. They are so open. They are sensitive and perceptive. Although this can be positive, it can also present a problem if the adults who work with them are not open and sensitive and perceptive.

How does one minister to children? Children's workers have a special opportunity in Sunday School or in other Christian educational opportunities. However, children's workers are not the only ones who have the opportunity to counsel children. Adult workers often have opportunity to minister to children.

Jerry and Dianne West had been married for eight years. They had two children, Boyd, age six and Somerlie, age four. One evening on the way home from work, Dianne was killed by a drunken driver. Beverly Sharpe, Dianne's Sunday School teacher, went immediately to the home when she learned of the accident. When she arrived, the pastor was there talking to Jerry. Beverly looked around for the children. She found them upstairs in one of the bedrooms all by themselves. They were frightened and crying. Beverly put her arms around them, and they began to sob even harder. For a few minutes they all cried together.

When they had quieted down some, she asked them what was wrong. Somerlie replied, "Daddy said Mommie was dead. He said she had gone on a long trip to see Jesus and was never coming back.

I don't want her to go see Jesus. I want her here. I don't like Jesus.
I want my Mommie."

"Yes," replied Beverly. "Your mother has died. A man who
shouldn't have been driving ran into your mother's car. I'm very sad
that she has died. I know it makes you sad, too. Jesus is also sad that
your mother has died."

"She wouldn't have been killed if I had emptied the trash like she
asked me to do," sobbed Boyd. "I really meant to do it."

"Boyd," Beverly said, "your mother was killed because a man was
driving who was not fit to drive. It had nothing to do with you. Even
if you had emptied the trash, it would not have kept the man from
running into your mother."

Beverly continued to sit with the children. Occasionally, one of
them would ask some question about death or about who was going
to take care of them now that their mother was dead. Beverly answered the questions as best she could, assuring the children that
their father loved them and that many other people did, too.

"When I think of your mother," Beverly said, "I think of how
pretty she looked last Sunday morning when she sang in church.
Somerlie, what is your favorite memory of your mother?" The children began the process of remembering the good things about their
mother. Soon the children's grandmother arrived, and Beverly turned
the children over to her. Because of her sensitivity, Beverly Sharpe
helped more than she will ever know. Her sensitivity enabled two
children to understand death and to feel comforted in the midst of
their fear. Would that all children could have someone that sensitive
at the time of tragedy in their lives.

Let's look at what Beverly Sharpe did right in her ministering.

She went immediately. She did not wait until later to go. Her
schedule allowed her to go immediately. That was the time she was
needed. Later, other friends and relatives would be present.

She didn't tell Jerry that if there was anything she could do to
please let her know. She looked for a need and sought to meet it. Even
if she had asked, it is unlikely the children's father would have even
thought of the children. In time of grief and death, look for something to do—don't ask.

She got down on the children's level physically. Because of her
previous relationship with the children, they gave her permission to

put her arms around them. This touching communicates even more than words.

She let the children cry. Not once did she tell them they should stop crying. Children, as well as adults, need to cry. They had lost one of the most important persons in their lives. Why shouldn't they cry? Tears have a way of helping us wash away our grief.

She let them express why they were crying. This is important. She did not know what the children knew. Were they crying just because their father was upset? Did they know their mother was dead? What had their father told them? In letting the children tell her what was wrong she learned the answer to these questions. It would not have been her place to tell the children their mother was dead if their father had not told them. That remains the right and responsibility of the parents.

She affirmed their mother's death and used the word *death* instead of a substitute. This is important in helping the children to accept that their mother was dead.

She did not overreact to Somerlie's statement that she didn't like Jesus. She accepted it for what it was—a statement made by a four-year-old who had lost her mother and who was scared, angry, and frightened. Beverly did tell the children that Jesus was sad, too.

She admitted her own grief and sadness. The children saw her cry. She demonstrated that it was all right to be sad at the time of loss.

She corrected Boyd's illogical association of his mother's death with his not emptying the trash. She was able to do this early in the grieving process before he had lived too long with the idea.

She let the children ask questions about death and what the future held. Whether she had all the answers or not was immaterial. She let them express their feelings without fear of criticism.

She shared her favorite memories of their mother and got the children to begin remembering the good things about their mother and talking about her.

She helped the children see that God was not the cause of their mother's death. Instead of saying that God had taken her, Beverly affirmed God's sadness at their mother's death. She did not make God the cause of their mother's death. She put the responsibility on the drunken driver, not God.

Children are people, too. They need to be cared for. Most of the suggestions given for ministering to adults discussed in chapters 3 and 4 can be applied to children. However, some special suggestions can help.

Guidelines for Counseling Children

Children See Through Insincerity

Adults can see through insincerity and phoniness, but children are especially perceptive. Be honest with them. Do not give them some phony story that is not true in an attempt to explain a difficult situation. Boyd and Somerlie's mother had not gone on a long trip. She had died. While children do not understand death the way adults do, they do understand. They have had pets die. They have seen people die on television. Be honest in what you tell children.

When a crisis involves an adult, the temptation is to deal with the adult and forget the children. Children feel that they do not count when they are not allowed to be a part of the process. Beverly Sharpe performed a special ministry because she was sensitive to the needs of the children. Their father was being cared for. The children's needs were as great as was their father's although in a different way. Often adults think they are doing children a favor by not talking about death in the children's presence. However, children, even as adults, need to verbalize their feelings.

Children Easily Blame Themselves

Children are not logical in their thinking. Boyd's conclusion that his mother was killed because he had not emptied the trash is typical of a child. Children are quick to assume that if they had only done something or not done something, a divorce or death would not have occurred. They need to be assured that nothing they did or did not do caused the tragedy.

Avoid Symbolism

Children often miss the symbolism that is helpful to adults. They take the symbolism literally. To explain a parent's death by saying that God looked around at all the beautiful flowers on earth and decided He wanted the child's parent to add to His bouquet will give the child a false concept of death as well as make God the cause of the parent's death.

Take Children Seriously

Children are not adults, nor should they be treated like adults. However, their feelings should be taken seriously. "They really don't understand; they're just children!" is a real fallacy. They do not understand like adults do, but they do understand far more than many adults think they do. Be as concerned with a child's feelings in the midst of a crisis as you are with an adult's. Again the Golden Rule may be applied. If you were a child, would you want people to pay attention to you? Would you want them to listen to you? Would you want someone to tell you it's all right to cry? Would you want someone to tell you what is going on in the event of a death or accident?

So do children. One should not go into all the minute details about a particular situation. If a couple is getting a divorce because Daddy was caught in bed with another woman, the children do not need all of the details. They don't need to be told that Daddy is going on a long trip and won't be back for a long time.

Children are people, too. Take them seriously.

Affirm Emotion

Assure children that it is all right to cry. They need to know that it is quite all right to cry if that is what they feel like doing. Something about crying does help wash away our grief. Jesus' weeping at the grave of Lazarus (John 11:35) has made weeping not only acceptable but honorable. If He could cry, who are we to tell children that they should not cry?

It's all right to be angry, too. A child may feel anger at God for letting his mother die. He may feel anger at the mother for having died. He may be angry at himself for having done or not having done something. That's OK. We always feel angry when we don't get what we want, when something denies us what we want. Why shouldn't children be angry when they lose a parent or a sibling, or something meaningful to them?

Parents and other adults can tell children that it is all right to show emotion at the time of a loss. However, the best way to communicate this message is to demonstrate it. "I've got to hold up for the children's sake," parents often say. Well-meaning friends tell parents, "Stop crying now; you don't want the children to see you this way." Why? What is wrong with children seeing a parent cry? Nothing! Children who have parents who model acceptable ways of expressing their grief are fortunate indeed.

Don't Place Unnecessary Burdens on Children

Bill had been only eight years old when his father dropped dead of a heart attack. During the funeral, several people came up to Bill and told him what a big boy he was and that he was going to have to take his daddy's place. Others told him that his mother was going to need his help now that his daddy was gone. No one ever talked to Bill about his father's death, and he began to think of himself as assuming his father's role.

One night a couple of weeks after the funeral he was missing his father greatly. He asked his mother if he could sleep in "daddy's place" in the bed, and his mother agreed. Soon he began sleeping with his mother regularly. His mother thought it "cute" the way Bill tried to immitate his father and praised him for helping her. This intensified Bill's desire to please his mother and to take his father's place.

Bill did not marry until he was in his early thirties. However, he had difficulty functioning as a sexual partner with his wife. After a great deal of therapy, Bill was able to see that he had never stopped trying to be the father to his mother and that he could never relate properly to his wife until he "buried" his father and assumed the role of husband to his wife.

Not all situations are as serious as Bill's, but it is unrealistic and dangerous to tell children that they have to take someone's place. They are children and were not meant to assume an adult's role. They need to relate to their parents as children, not as adults. They need to relate to other brothers and sisters as siblings, not as parents. They need to be able to grieve as children and not have the unreal expectations of adulthood forced on them. At this point in their lives they do not have the equipment to handle adult responsibilities.

Get Down on the Child's Level

Can you imagine what a world filled with kneecaps looks like? If so, you can picture a world from a young child's perspective. Everything looks big to a child. Most adults have had the experience of going back to a place in their childhood and seeing a building or other object that they had imagined to be much bigger as a child. In one sense, it was much bigger. Compared to the height of the child, it was about twice as big as it would be when compared to that same person as an adult.

When you talk with a child, try to place yourself on the same level as the child. This may mean kneeling down as you talk. If the children are young enough and give you permission, you might be able to place them on your lap. Whatever is necessary, try to talk to the children from their level, not from the heights of adulthood.

Counseling for Conversion

Counseling children about accepting Christ is a significant part of the counseling process. Children, as adults, are not things to be manipulated; they are persons to be ministered to with all the compassion of Christ. As in all areas, Jesus is our example.

The occasion when parents brought their children to Jesus (Luke 18:15-17) provides us with some guidelines. In all likelihood, the children brought to Jesus were younger than those we normally think of as being old enough to make a profession of faith in Christ. However, Jesus' attitude toward them would also be His attitude toward children who come to trust Him as personal Savior: "Let the children come to me and do not stop them, because the Kingdom of God belongs to such as these" (Luke 18:16, GNB).

Children have a great faith. They can believe when adults cannot. Because of this great faith, those who would seek to lead children to a knowledge of Christ must be careful. Children can be manipulated into making statements that they really do not believe.

Adults can put undue pressure on children to make "religious" decisions. Such pressure should be avoided at all cost.

Bessie Bedford had taught third and fourth graders for more years than anyone could remember. During all those years she had not had a child come through her department who had not made a public profession of faith. Her pastors often held her up as an example of evangelistic concern for all Sunday School workers.

The children enjoyed her teaching. She did a lot activities with them and regularly had them in her home for parties. One year the pastor's son was in her department. This placed additional responsibility on her to maintain her record. Just before the fourth graders moved to the fifth grade department, she invited all of the children to her home for a picnic. After the fun and games, she talked to the group and told them how much she cared for them and would miss them. Then she reminded them that she had never had anyone who had been in her department who had left without making a public profession of faith. She asked those who had not done so if they would make that decision right now to help her keep her record going. She asked them all to bow their heads and pray a prayer after her. They did, then she pronounced that they were all now Christians and should present themselves to the church Sunday morning for membership and baptism.

Regardless of how much children like someone or how much they would like for her to keep a record going, neither of these reasons is adequate to justify making a profession of faith. There is no faith in Jesus to profess. It is faith in a teacher more than in a loving Savior. The children have not believed in Jesus; they have expressed their love for a teacher and responded to peer pressure.

Salvation is the most important decision one will ever make. That decision must be made only under the leadership of the Holy Spirit, not under undue pressure of a kind Sunday School worker.

What can be done? No one knows when a child is ready to make a profession of faith. Children mature at different rates. Each child is an individual. Children must understand that they are sinners in need of a Savior before salvation can occur. This does not mean being sorry they disobeyed Mother and Daddy. Seeing themselves as sinners means seeing themselves separated from God because of their sin. This understanding will come to different children at different ages. In most cases, it will come around the age of puberty. Sunday School workers should not ignore children, nor should pressure be put on children to make a decision that will not be valid. Children should be nurtured and encouraged to let Jesus help them live daily as He wants them to do.

Sunday School workers can share Christ's love for the children they teach. They can answer questions children ask. They can share how much God loves them by teaching about the cross in a positive way, without playing on the sympathies of the children. The pastor can be invited to share with the children in a context of openness and understanding where they have the opportunity to ask questions and to get acquainted with the pastor.

Sunday School workers should be cautious about using the "language of Zion." Many of these terms are meaningful to adults, but they have a completely different meaning to children. Be sure you "translate" religious terms into language children understand.

The encourager role of Sunday School workers is at its peak in leading anyone to know Christ as Savior. Especially is this true when the workers have the opportunity of leading a child who has a whole life to give to Christ. We certainly have no right to "forbid them" (Luke 18:16) from coming to Jesus; neither do we have any right to coerce them. As always, follow Jesus' example if in doubt. You will not be wrong.

Illness and Hospitalization

Hospitalization and illness are always difficult times. Adults have special concerns (Who's going to take care of the children? Who's going to do my work while I'm sick? How will I pay the bill?). Children, too, have special concerns. They are not the same concerns that adults have, but they are as real to the child as adult concerns are to them. Children's workers can help alleviate some of these concerns and make the illness or hospitalization less upsetting.

Max Price, in his excellent series of pamphlets "Helping Children Cope" (see bibliography), has one pamphlet on illness and hospitalization. The pamphlet is written for parents and is designed to be handed to parents before a child enters the hospital. Although the children's worker will not be able to do those things for the child that parents should do, the workers will have opportunity to counsel with parents of the children who are in their department.

Price lists five suggestions to help ease the emotional stress of hospitalization and illness: (1) Allow the child time to prepare for hospitalization when possible. (2) Include the child in his own treatment as far as possible. (3) To the best of your knowledge, give the child all the information he asks. (4) Allow the child to take some items from home to the hospital to help the child feel more secure. (5) Treat the child as normal as possible. Do not let a sick child get by with inappropriate behavior just because he is sick. Parents who provide consistent discipline for a sick child aid in the child's healing.

Even if children's workers are not able to minister to the parents before a child enters the hospital, they still can do many things to help the child in a difficult situation.

Visit Prior to Hospitalization

Children's trips to the hospital are not always planned, but when a worker finds out about such a trip, a visit in the home the day before the child enters the hospital can indicate to the child that you are interested. It can help establish contact with the child and establish a bridge between the strange world of the hospital and the world the child normally lives in. You might take a copy of a book like *Curious George Goes to the Hospital* (see bibliography) for the child and a copy of "Helping Children Cope with Illness and Hospitalization" for the parents.

Visit Child in the Hospital

Visiting a child in the hospital will help the child feel that people have not deserted him. In the teaching period on Sunday, the teachers have often taught about how much God cares for the children. Now they have an opportunity to demonstrate that concern.

Obey Hospital Rules

Most, if not all of the suggestions for visiting the sick mentioned in chapter 6 also apply to visiting children. Study these suggestions carefully.

Send Letters and Cards from Children

If possible, let the children make cards or write letters to their friends in the hospital. These cards and letters from friends their own age can be a real source of encouragement.

Offer to Stay with the Child

Many children need someone with them around the clock. Parents, who have to work and do not have grandparents or other relatives nearby, might appreciate an offer to sit with the child while they run errands, work, or get some much-needed sleep. This offer might be especially appreciated in the case of a single parent. If parents do not want to leave, the Sunday School worker might be able to run certain errands for them.

Listen

In visiting children who are sick at home or in the hospital, one of the most important ministries an encourager can perform is to listen to the child. Children need to talk. They do not understand the world logically. They may not understand many of the procedures being performed on them at the hospital. Workers can listen to them and possibly relieve some anxiety and frustration.

Divorce

Divorce creates many problems. Many of these problems involve the children. Frequently, they are the ones most often overlooked.

I asked a friend who had recently gone through a divorce what Sunday School workers could do to encourage children whose parents were divorced. The following suggestions are based on her comments.

Basic to the following suggestions is the relationship the worker has with the child. A worker who expects to teach children by coming to church on Sunday morning only will be a failure. Children need to feel special. One way of doing this is by visiting in their homes. Workers who have done this as well as sought other ways of getting acquainted with the children will be in a position to minister to children who are involved in divorce.

Do Not Label

Labels can be so damaging. Labels can affect a child for life. Children who are going through a divorce have enough problems and emotional needs without having to wear a label. Do not expect a child from a divorced home to act or react in any certain way. Generalizations that children from a divorced home will act in a certain manner is prejudice as much as prejudice against a person of another race. We ought not prejudge anyone, least of all children, by giving them labels.

Be a Friend

Children—especially older children—may need someone outside the family to be a special friend during this time. Parents are involved. Relatives often do not know how to respond to children. A caring worker-counselor may be able to fill a needed place in the life of a child at this time. Workers cannot take the place of parents, but they can substitute for them during this period in the child's life. Children need to know that adults care for them. Their parents may be so emotionally drained that they cannot provide all of the adult relationships children need. Children need someone who will listen to them and let them express their fears and grief without condemning or turning their backs on them.

Help Build a Good Self-Image

As in a death, children going through a divorce often pick up false signals and blame themselves for what has happened to their parents. Children need to be reassured that their actions had nothing at all to do with their parents' divorce. Worker-counselors can correct this misconception and help the children to see that their parents' problems do not make the children lesser persons.

Some of this reassuring can be done in the classroom; some will have to be done in personal conversation. A worker who knows the children will be able to involve children in the teaching session. Calling on them for answers, asking them to help with special projects, inviting them to go visit another child with you can help build self-esteem in a child. This personal attention says to the children that an adult cares for them at this point when the two most significant adults in their life are emotionally (and possibly physically) separated from them.

Treat Children Individually

Somehow we tend to herd children. We group them together and try to treat them all alike. I have often heard parents say, "I don't know why George turned out that way. We treated him just like we did all the other children." Therein lay the problem. George was not like the other children, and he did not need to be treated like them. He was an individual.

All children of divorce are not alike anymore than all children of married couples are alike. Yet we often tend to group them together and treat them as though they were all clones.

Some children are private persons and may need to be given privacy. It may be possible to verbalize what the children may be feeling and then to check it out with them as a way of helping them express their feelings. Other children are more open and need someone who will let them talk about their feelings. What will help one child cope will not work with another child.

Accept Children's Insecurity

Divorce can create insecurity in a child. This insecurity can come out in many different ways.

Missey was eight when Caroline and Steve divorced. The family had always gone to church, and Caroline continued to bring Missey to her same Sunday School. However, it became more difficult to get Missey to go. She just did not want to leave her mother and go in the Sunday School Department. Because of Caroline's sensitivity and good relationship with Missey, she was able to talk to her about it. She asked Missey if she were afraid she would not come back to get her after church. Missey acknowledged that she was afraid of that, and her mother assured Missey that she would never do that to her daughter. Having talked about the situation helped Missey to put her insecurity into words and then work through it.

Worker-counselors who work with children need to be especially sensitive to these feelings of insecurity following a period of divorce. This may last for many months or even years.

Don't Pity the Children

Children of divorce need many things, but pity is not needed. Yes, it is sad that their parents have not been able to live together. Yes, it is sad because of the hurt in the lives of all the people involved. However, trying to minister to children from a "oh-you-poor-deprived-child" attitude will not win the children's confidence.

Be open and admit your sympathy over the situation. Then, by your attitude and action, help the child move forward to accept the reality (and finality) of the situation and get on with living.

6
Some Special Considerations

The range of problems worker-counselors will encounter is unlimited. Some are so out of the ordinary that the encourager will not have any experience in dealing with them. Other problems will surface again and again.

Three problem areas deserve special consideration because they occur frequently and because of the magnitude of the problem. Each of these areas requires much more help than can be given in a brief chapter. All that can be done is to point in the right direction. Consult the bibliography for more detailed help in each of these areas.

The Ministry to the Sick

Ministering to the sick may be the most frequent ministry encouragers will perform. Most people are sick at some point in their lives. Few people are able to go for long without a stay in the hospital or an illness at home. Ministering to those who are ill is an essential part of an encourager's ministry.

Even though most people will experience a serious illness at some point in their lives, few people feel comfortable about visiting in the hospital or visiting a sick person at home. The following guidelines will offer some suggestions to make your visiting more beneficial to the patient and more comfortable for you.

Obey Visiting Hours

Visiting hours are established for a purpose. A set time when visitors can see patients helps both the patient and the staff. Visiting hours differ from hospital to hospital. Check with each hospital and abide by their schedules. When it comes to visiting hours, you are not special. Patients' needs are more important than your schedule.

Obey Signs

Hospitals place many signs on doors and in rooms. These signs are posted for good reasons. They are a way of helping the patients in those rooms get well. Such signs as "No Visitors," "Isolation," "Nothing by Mouth" are all intended to communicate a message to hospital staff and visitors. Worker-counselors have no right to assume that the signs apply to others but do not apply to them.

Keep Your Visits Brief

No set length of time can be established for a hospital visit. Every visit is dependent upon the patient. At times you may drive across town and enter a patient's room only to find the patient is too sick for a visit. In that case, a one-minute visit may be long enough. If a person is about to go home, is not seriously ill, and feels like talking, you probably would stay longer. How well you know the patient also affects the length of your visit. A good average may be five—seven minutes. It would be better to err on the side of brevity than to stay too long.

Knock if the Door Is Closed

If the door to a patient's room is closed, always knock before entering. Failure to do so can embarrass the patient and visitor. If the light is on over the door, check at the nurses' station before entering. The patient has some need that should be cared for before having visitors. The patient may need some pain medication, may need to have the bed adjusted, or may need to have a bedpan removed. In any case, a visit at that time would hurt more than help.

Position Yourself for the Patient's Benefit

When you enter a room, stand or sit (I normally prefer to stand.) so the patient does not have to strain to see you. This may mean standing at the foot of the bed. Make it easy on the patient. Most patients will offer you a seat. If the patient is lying flat of his back and can only look upward, you would not want to sit.

Do Not Give Food Without Permission

A simple gesture of goodwill can become dangerous. A patient who has just been diagnosed as having diabetes does not need her favorite milkshake. The safest procedure is to stop by the nurses' station and ask if the patient can have some particular food or drink.

Do Not Sit on the Bed

Sitting on or even bumping the patient's bed can cause pain. Someone who is in pain from surgery or who has a headache can be made very uncomfortable if you even bump into the bed. Be careful about wires and cords affixed to the bed. Also the hand-held urinals are often hung on the side of the bed after they have been used for the nurse to pick up. They can be knocked off—as this writer once discovered to his embarrassment!

Be Observant

Upon entering the room you can learn a great deal. Learn to look. Does the patient have flowers, cards, baskets of fruit? A patient who has been in the hospital for a week and does not have any cards may be lonely. Is there a tray sitting nearby with only a few bites of food gone? Be sensitive to these signs.

Watch Your Conversation

Your purpose for visiting is to help the patient. Many patients would have been better off without some visits.

WOULD-BE-ENCOURAGER: You have the same illness my mother had.

PATIENT: Really? What happened to her?

WOULD-BE ENCOURAGER: She died last year.

This is not much of an exaggeration. Never mind that the mother may have been killed in a car accident. The damage has been done. Be cautious what you say.

Don't Play Doctor or Nurse

Remember, you are an encourager, not a doctor or nurse. Stick to your role and let the medical team do theirs. Don't read the charts, check the monitor, or take the patient's temperature. I prefer not even to ask patients how they are feeling. In the hospital that is a medical question. As an encourager you cannot do anything if the patient says he has a severe pain in his side. Your purpose in your visit is to brighten the person's day, not diagnose his illness nor prescribe treatment.

Let the Patient Offer to Shake Hands

A patient may not want to shake hands for many reasons. Sometimes a person may have received an intravenous solution through her hand, and her hand may be sore. Older persons may have arthritis. Whatever the reason, let the patient be the one to initiate the hand-shaking ritual. When you do shake hands, do so gently.

Speak in a Moderate Voice

One does not need to whisper in a hospital room. Nor should one speak so loudly the person next door benefits (?) from your visit. Whispering makes the patients wonder if you know something they don't. Whispering to family members or nurses in the patient's hearing can especially create suspicion on the patient's part. You may be talking about the score of last night's ball game, but the patients will think you are talking about them.

Don't Visit When You Are Sick

Martyrdom may have its place, but it is not in hospital visiting. If you are sick, stay home. You can call or write a letter. If you are not well, you stand a chance of giving the patient something. Too, you are more susceptible to picking up illnesses from the hospital yourself if your defenses are not up to par.

Speak to Other Patients if Convenient

If other patients occupy the room with the person you are visiting, speak to them if it is convenient. Often the person you are visiting will introduce you to the other patients. By all means, don't awaken another patient or disturb one who appears to be critically ill.

Use Prayer and Scripture Wisely

At times one may have difficulty in knowing when to use Scripture and prayer. No one rule can cover all situations. Some people want you to pray and read the Bible; others definitely do not want you to do it. I normally do not like to visit with a big Bible in my hand. I like to carry a pocket New Testament and Psalms. Your favorite book store has many good, inexpensive Scripture portions that make excellent handouts for hospital visitation. Instead of reading the Bible, you might want to leave a Scripture portion for the patient to read later.

Prayer can also be offered in several different ways. You can ask the patients if there is anything they want you to do before you leave. Some people do not want someone offering public prayer for them. Remember, your purpose is to help the patient rather than to offer prayer. You can speak your prayer for the person if the situation does not lend itself to verbal prayer. You can say something like the following: "I want you to know that I am praying for you. My prayer is that you will be able to be out of the hospital and back to work soon." You might also volunteer to express gratitude for the food if the patient's tray is brought during your visit.

Be sensitive to praying and reading the Bible. Let the Holy Spirit use you to mediate His comfort and help to troubled people. The care you demonstrate at this point can open many opportunities for a later ministry.

Listen

The hospital room is a good place to listen. Often patients will want to talk. They have concerns and anxieties that may require a listening ear. Here is one place you can practice the ministry of listening. Let the patient talk. Don't feel that you have to share a similar experience. Pray for the Holy Spirit's guidance that He will enable you to know when to talk and when to listen.

Don't Have a Party in the Room

Many hospitals limit the number of visitors in a room at one time to two or three. If you encounter a situation where four or five persons are present, speak a word of greeting and tell the patient that you will be back later. And then leave.

Leave a Message if the Patient Is Not In

If you should happen to make a visit when patients are out of the room, by all means leave a note telling them you were there. If you can come back later, mention that. If not, tell them you will check with them later. Then be sure you do whatever you say.

Don't Criticize the Medical Team

Whatever you do, do not criticize the medical team. They are not perfect, of course, but they may be doing something or not doing something for good reasons. The last thing patients need is for someone to raise doubts about the quality of medical help they are getting.

Be Cheerful

Most people in the hospital have enough problems without having to experience the gloom brought in from the outside. You may feel like the world is caving in upon you—and it may be—but if you can't bring a bit of cheer to a hospital room, then you should stay away. Be positive and upbeat about what you have to say.

Hospital visitation is more of an art than a science. No one can memorize a rule to cover every situation. All we can do is try to be sensitive to the patient's needs and pray that the Holy Spirit will lead us faithfully to represent Jesus Christ in this situation in helping the patient in some way.

Follow-up visitation after the patient leaves the hospital is also important. In fact, this is one area where worker-counselors can provided a much-needed ministry. Few pastors and/or church staff members have the time to do follow-up visitation after people leave the hospital. Worker-counselors can provide a ministry of great value by visiting after the patient is home. Telephone calls, cards, and letters from class members can be a source of comfort.

A class member who is ill and cannot attend or who is involved in a long convalescence requires a special ministry. It is easy to forget about people who are confined at home.

Our class had a member who was unable to climb the stairs to our room, so we occasionally went to his home to meet with him. We would meet about thirty minutes earlier than we did at church, and we left early enough to get to the worship service on time. It was a good experience for him and for us.

Ministry to the physically ill is an opportunity to meet people's needs and to be encouragers in the fullest sense of that word.

Death and Grief

A second area that worker-counselors encounter regularly is the area of death and grief. Death is such a terrible event. It is final. It is not something the dying get to practice for. It is an end.

Yet, it is at this point that our Christian faith speaks most completely. If our faith has no word at this point, it is useless.

In recent years, a great deal of work has been done on understanding the process of grief one passes through in dealing with death. Some understanding of this process is imperative to the worker-counselor who would be an encourager at the time of death and grief.

The most complete work of understanding the stages through which we go when we are dying is Elisabeth Kübler-Ross's *On Death and Dying.* Her book is significant because it clearly and concisely identifies five stages through which we go in accepting our own death. These stages are (1) denial and isolation, (2) anger, (3) bargaining, (4) depression, and (5) acceptance.[1] Others have suggested somewhat different breakdowns of the stages, but, basically, they are similar: We deny we are going to die; we get angry because we know it is true; we try to bargain with God and others; we get depressed; and then, hopefully, we accept the fact.

Not all people pass through these stages in a logical, neat manner. Some may stay at one stage longer than others. Some may never come to accept the fact that they are going to die.

How does an encourager relate to someone who is terminally ill? Very carefully! It requires all of our wisdom and knowledge plus all the leadership of the Holy Spirit. Worker-counselors would do well to be familiar with the five stages of death. People are not robots, and they cannot be lumped into specific categories. However, these categories are broad enough that they will normally fit most people who have terminal illnesses.

Ray was an inactive member of a men's Sunday School class. He had not been present for well over a year. One Sunday morning he showed up for Sunday School early. He had a new Bible under his arm. During the Bible study, he participated freely.

After the class ended, he lingered for a while and walked out with the teacher. "I suppose you are wondering why I'm here this morning," he said. "I have had quite a shock this past week. I went to the doctor, and he said that I had cancer. I went back to the office and got down on my knees by my desk and promised the Lord that if He would heal me that I would never miss another Sunday at church. I felt a surge of something pass through my body. It was almost like a wave of intense light. I just know I am healed, and I'm going to live up to my part of the bargain."

Ray had jumped quickly to the bargaining stage. It is not at all unusual for someone to try to strike a bargain with God. How do worker-counselors handle this kind of response? Again, very carefully! One cannot say that God has not healed Ray. That is God's decision. He can do anything He wants. However, if God has healed Ray, it is not because he agreed to go to church every Sunday.

Ray's teacher, Jim Henderson, expressed his sorrow that Ray had been diagnosed as having cancer. He then expressed his gratitude for the experience Ray had described which he had had with God. However, he also encouraged Ray to keep in close contact with the doctor. He suggested that God might choose to heal Ray through the use of the doctor's skill. Ray agreed, but he was certain that God had already removed the malignancy from his body.

The next Sunday Ray was back. Again he participated in the Bible study. At one point he shared his experience with the whole class. "I am convinced that God has healed me so I can be a witness to His healing power. I am willing to go anywhere at anytime to tell people what the Lord has done for me."

Jim watched Ray carefully over the next several weeks. Ray appeared to be losing weight. Occasionally, Jim would stop by Ray's house and visit with him. Ray was always so optimistic. He never gave the slightest indication that he did not believe the Lord had healed him.

One Sunday Ray was not at church. Jim called him that afternoon. Ray's wife answered the phone. She said Ray was sick and in bed. Then she confided in Jim that Ray had been sick several days recently, and that she was quite concerned. He had also begun to find some lumps in the same area where the doctor had removed the growth earlier.

Later that week Jim got word that Ray had been hospitalized. He stopped by the next afternoon to visit him. Ray was still quite exuberant. "Well, the doctors said that the cancer has come back. But you and I know better, don't we? God's just testing my faith. I know He still has plans for me."

Jim assured Ray of God's love for him, prayed with him, and left. Later that week he stopped back to see Ray. This time Ray did not greet Jim with his usual enthusiasm. When Jim asked if he had had a good day, Ray exploded. "How can I have a good day when the doctors tell me I'm dying. I overheard them tell my wife that I don't have but about three weeks to live. I feel that God has really let me down. All that garbage in the Bible about God answering prayers just isn't true. He did not heal me. And I never missed a Sunday up until last week. I had even started tithing. And this is how He repays me!"

Jim listened to Ray talk for a while. Then he said, "Ray, I know you are upset. I do not understand why God heals some but does not heal others. All I know is that He cares very much for you. He understands and hurts with you."

At this stage of Ray's illness, he was experiencing some anger as well as depression. He had tried to bargain with God, and the bargain did not work. This was a crucial time in his life. Whether he came to grips with his illness and dealt with those matters that one needs to take care of before one dies depended on his response at this point. In Ray's case, his illness developed quite rapidly. He never had time to deal with his anger, and he died, leaving a frustrated wife and family.

Could Jim have done anything more than he did? Probably not. A more experienced counselor may have gotten through the veneer Ray had built around accepting his illness. However, people will only hear what they want to hear. Ray never accepted the fact that he had cancer until it was too late for him to deal with it.

All situations we encounter are not successful. We cannot force people to respond like we want them to. All we can do is support and minister to them to the best of our abilities.

Grief

What about those who are left behind when someone like Ray dies? How do we minister to those who are grieving?

As there are various stages persons pass through in their dying, grieving persons also pass through different stages. In his excellent book *Dealing with Death: A Christian Perspective,* D. P. Brooks suggests five stages a grieving person goes through: (1) shock and unbelief, (2) numbness, (3) flood of grief, (4) rebuilding, and (5) return to new life.[2]

Encouragers will benefit from being aware that a grieving person passes through certain stages. Again, these stages are not absolute and rigid, but they do offer a framework that will help us understand grief.

Grief can come from many different experiences. Death certainly is one of these. But a divorce, a child leaving home, the death of a pet, the loss of a job, a move, an amputation can all cause grief.

While I was a pastor, one of our regular families did not come to church on Sunday. I visited them during the week and found that their dog had been run over and killed just as they were getting ready to come to church. They had all stayed home that morning because they were too upset to come to church. I remember thinking that was rather unnecessary. This past fall I had the responsibility of taking our standard schnauzer, Willie, whom we had had for fourteen years, to the vet to have him put to sleep. I am much more sympathetic with this family whose dog was killed. A couple of my collegues at work recently put their pets to sleep and experienced the same feelings I had. Remember that grief can stem from any loss.

Unresolved grief causes as many difficulties in our lives as any one other problem. We are afraid to grieve. We do so much to keep from admitting our grief. When we experience a loss, it is very real. C. S. Lewis, in his insightful book *A Grief Observed* described the experience of working through his grief when his wife died. "No one ever told me that grief felt so like fear. I am not afraid, but the sensation is like being afraid. The same fluttering in the stomach, the same restlessness, the yawning. I keep on swallowing."[3]

A little later he wrote: "Getting over it so soon? But the words are ambiguous. To say the patient is getting over it after an operation for appendicitis is one thing; after he's had his leg off it is quite another. . . . At present I am learning to get about on crutches. Perhaps I shall presently be given a wooden leg. But I shall never be a biped again."[4]

Grief is real. Never take it lightly or try to deny it. The best ministry an encourager can have in the face of grief is to accept the reality and painfulness of the loss and be present to listen to the person who is grieved.

The following suggestions should help one deal with someone who is grieving.

Acknowledge That the Grief Is Real

Whatever the loss, acknowledge that the grief is real. A child may have lost a pet. A man may have lost a job. A wife may have lost her husband. Each loss is real to the person involved. Don't tell the people they should not feel the way they do.

Don't deny people's feelings. Great damage can be done by a failure to acknowledge the realness of grief. Often well-meaning people will say "Now, you mustn't feel that way!" as though telling them will change the way they feel. All that it will do is keep them from expressing to us (or possibly others) how they feel and prevent their working through their grief.

Listen—Let the People Talk

In dealing with grieving people, the first suggestion for counseling can be applied with great benefit—listen, listen, listen! Let the people talk about how they feel. Don't try to stop them. It helps—not hurts—to let people talk about their loss.

A friend who had recently undergone open heart surgery shared with me an insightful observation. He said that people who have had open heart surgery go through a period of depression. When I asked why, he hesitated for a moment and then replied: "In open heart surgery you are face-to-face with death, and nobody will let you talk about it."

Whatever the source of grief may be, let people talk. Listen to them.'

Talk About the Loss Yourself

Talk about the loss in your conversation with the grieving person. Often people feel that the best thing they can do is to avoid bringing up the subject. Wrong! Most people who have experienced a loss want to talk about the loss. That is the best therapy for working through grief.

Keep in Touch

Keep in contact with the grieving people. Stop by and visit. Call. Go out to lunch. Invite them over for a meal. Don't avoid them. Especially is this true in the case of a divorce or death.

God's presence through the Holy Spirit is available even when we do not feel His presence. He strengthens and comforts us. William P. Tuck points out that the word *comfort* comes from two words *com*, "with" plus *fortis*, "strength."[5] When Isaiah declared, "Comfort ye"

(Isa. 40:1), he was saying, "Strengthen ye." "The comfort which comes from the abiding Presence of God is an inner strength which fortifies us to face any situation because we are aware that we do not confront it isolated and alone."[6]

God will help those who grieve. The only ones He cannot help are those who will not admit their hurt.

Divorce

In browsing through a card shop I was surprised to come upon two nearly identical cards side by side. Both pictured wedding cakes with the traditional bride and groom on them. Inside one the message read, "Congratulations on your marriage." However, the other card had the groom turned upside down with his face covered with cake (was the symbolism accidental?). Inside the verse read, "Congratulations on your divorce!"

OK, I didn't like it either, but how do we relate to people who have gone through a divorce? We may not want to send a card, but sending a card would be better than ignoring the situation altogether.

Divorce is a time for grieving, just as is death. Those involved have experienced loss and pain; they have also experienced the silence of the community. At least at the time of death, we can send cards or flowers or write a brief note expressing our sympathy. But how do we relate to someone who has recently divorced or is in the process? The suggestions about dealing with grief would apply to ministering to a divorced person. In addition, the following should also be considered.

Acknowledge the Divorce

Before you can begin to minister to a person who has been divorced, or is in the process of getting a divorce, you must openly acknowledge the fact of the divorce. Express your sorrow to the person that is going through the divorce. If you cannot do this face-to-face, you can write a note to the person. Acknowledging the divorce opens up the opportunity for ministry.

Don't Judge—Leave That to God

It is difficult not to judge whether a person is right or wrong in getting a divorce. But that is not the job of an encourager. Judgment belongs exclusively to God. Whatever your personal feelings are about divorce, a judgmental attitude toward divorced persons will cut off any potential ministry.

Don't Let Your Theology Hinder Your Ministry

Divorce is a divisive issue. Many churches and pastors take a strong stand against divorce. Before encouragers can minister to divorced persons, they must work through their feelings about divorce. Divorce is always a failure. It is an admission on the part of two supposedly mature adults that they could not make a success of their relationship. Just because that is true, those who are involved in a divorce need support and comfort. We have all failed in many areas of our lives. Although a failure in marriage is significant, our Lord Christ is able to forgive. Encouragers can communicate that word of forgiveness and the accompanying word of hope.

Include the People in Social Engagements

Don't cut divorced people off from social engagements. They still have social needs. Most of our social functions center around couples. It is easy to ignore divorced persons as well as those who are widowed when extending invitations to social activities. Extend the invitation, and let the persons decide if they would feel comfortable in attending. Plan social occasions that do not emphasize couples.

Few encouragers will feel comfortable in ministering in any of these three areas—sickness, death and grief, and divorce. No set of suggestions can ever make one feel completely at ease. These suggestions are nudges in the right direction. Familiarize yourself with them. Be sensitive to people's needs. Empathize with them. Empathy is putting yourself in their shoes. Ask yourself what you would want someone to do if you were in that situation. In the final analysis, that is really putting into practice the Golden Rule: minister to others as you would want them to minister to you if you were in that situation.

Notes
1. Elisabeth Kübler-Ross, *On Death and Dying* (New York: The Macmillan Company, 1969).

2. D. P. Brooks, *Dealing with Death: A Christian Perspective* (Nashville: Broadman Press, 1974).

3. C. S. Lewis, *A Grief Observed* (New York: Seabury Press, 1961), p. 7.

4. Ibid., p. 43.

5. William P. Tuck, *Facing Grief* and *Death* (Nashville: Broadman Press, 1975), p. 41.

6. Ibid.

7
The Ministry of Referral

Worker-counselors often encounter situations they are unable to handle for one reason or other. The worker simply may not have the time to deal with the request. The nature of the need may lie beyond the worker-counselor's ability. The nature of the situation may make the worker-counselor feel uncomfortable.

Martha Mills was walking out of the classroom one Sunday morning following a lesson on the Christian view of marriage and divorce. As she walked out the door, Bob and Nancy Bates were standing in the middle of the hall. Both of them had been in her couples' class that morning. She spoke to them and started to hurry on to the choir. Bob caught hold of her arm and said, "Martha, you raised some interesting questions this morning. I wonder if you would come by the house some evening so we could talk?" Martha agreed that she would call them to set up a time, and she went on to the choir.

That afternoon, she called and arranged for a visit on Monday evening. When she arrived, Bob said, "Martha, you said some things Sunday morning I wanted to talk to you about. As I understood you, you said that divorce was wrong. I agree with you, but Nancy does not. She told me last week that she wants a divorce. I've told her that the Bible says it is wrong, but she won't listen to me. Will you tell her that it's wrong?"

Martha looked at Nancy who had not said a word. She was angry and looked daggers at Bob for having put her on the spot that way.

Martha realized what a difficult situation she was in. She smiled and said, "Well, Bob, you have certainly put me in a difficult spot. I do not want to take sides in a family quarrel because I care about both of you. Nancy, suppose you tell me what you're feeling right now."

With that, Nancy began to unload her hostility. She accused Bob of being overbearing, insensitive, and failing to understand her feelings.

Bob responded by accusing Nancy of being a terrible housekeeper, of paying more attention to all the other men instead of to him.

Martha realized that Bob and Nancy had some serious problems in their marriage, and that while neither seemingly wanted a divorce, something had to be done. After they had talked for a while, she asked them if they had seen anyone for counseling.

"We went to see Pastor Maguire, but he just told us to pray about the matter and come to church more. That didn't seem to do any good."

"I'm sorry you had such an experience with the pastor. However, other competent counselors are available who can help you. I have a friend who works at the county counseling center downtown that I recommend highly. I know him quite well and know him to be a committed Christian. I feel you have some needs that I can't meet. I would like to give you his name and suggest you call him and make an appointment. If it would be all right, I would be glad to call him and tell him you are going to contact him. I could share with him some of what you have shared with me today. That way, he would be expecting you. Would that be all right?"

Martha Miller had found herself in a difficult situation. It was a situation which lay beyond her skills. It was also a situation where she stood to lose the Bates's friendship because of the personal nature of the conflict. However, she cared about both Bob and Nancy. They had already tried one counselor, but because Martha had done her homework, she knew another of the great many resources in the community that were available. Martha was able to refer the couple to someone who could bring some skillful guidance to their relationship.

Referral is an important—yet difficult—aspect of the worker-counselor's ministry. It is not just getting rid of people because you don't want to help them or are unable to help them. It is putting them in touch with the resources available to them. In this sense, the worker-counselor is like a switchboard operator who is able to link a caller from outside with a person on the inside of the building who can provide the caller with the help and information needed.

When to Refer?

When does a worker-counselor need to refer someone? The situations in which worker-counselors should refer are many and varied. At times they may refer because of the worker-counselor's own situation. At other times, it may be because of the nature of the conflict.

Lack of Time

Time is a precious ingredient in our lives. We all have our own families and responsibilities to care for. We have to work. We have to meet our needs for rest. As great as our desire to help someone may be, we can get so overloaded that we simply cannot do justice to helping others without doing damage to ourselves.

Saying no when someone asks us for help is not wrong, if we do not have time to help. This does not mean we do not care. It really means just the opposite. It means that we do care, and we want them to receive the best help possible which, at the moment, will have to come from someone else.

If on a Sunday evening, a worker-counselor discovers someone who needs a job, and the worker is going to be out of town all week on a business trip, he would certainly need to refer the person to someone else who could help.

Lack of Ability

Ours is a complex world. No one can know everything about everything. Often during the day we encounter problems we cannot handle, and we ask for help. If our car suddenly develops an unexplainable thump-thump, we call a mechanic. If the plumbing breaks down, we call the plumber. If we develop a severe pain in the chest, we see the doctor.

Worker-counselors will encounter many situations that lie beyond their ability to help. Do not feel bad about that. It is worse to try to help and end up by hurting.

When we do encounter such situations, we need to put the person in touch with someone who can provide the help needed.

Sickness—Physical or Mental

If someone is physically sick—or thinks he is—then a medical doctor ought to be called in. Under no circumstances should the worker-counselor try to diagnose physical ailments.

If someone is not eating or sleeping or complains about pains in any part of her body, the person needs to see a doctor. If the person is unable to pay the cost of medical care, clinics are available in most cities where the person can receive free or lower-cost medical help.

Pregnancy—especially a pregnancy that occurs outside of the marriage relationship—is a peculiar need. Most communities have good clinics where both prenatal care for the baby and psychological care for the mother can be received. If need be, information about giving the baby up for adoption can also be provided.

Of course, a person who demonstrates any psychotic symptoms should be referred to a medical doctor. If a person is threatening suicide or threatening to kill someone else, the threat should always be taken seriously.

In the book *A Cry for Help* the authors list sixteen warning signals for teenagers who may be contemplating suicide. Many of these would apply to persons of all ages:

1. Acting out: aggressive, hostile behavior
2. Alcohol and drug abuse
3. Passive behavior
4. Changes in eating habits
6. Fear of separation
7. Abrupt changes in personality
8. Sudden mood swings
9. Impulsiveness
10. Slackening interest in schoolwork and decline in grades
11. Inability to concentrate
12. Loss or lack of friends
13. Loss of an important person or thing in the child's life
14. Hopelessness
15. Obsession with death: a death wish
16. Evidence that the child is making a will[1]

Suicide, especially among the young, is increasing at an alarming rate. At a minimum, fifty-seven American children and teens attempt suicide every hour.[2] This figure is based on hospital emergency room records. Since many attempted suicides are disguised as something else or not treated by emergency rooms, the figure is certainly much higher. The incidence of suicide has increased by as much as 3,000 percent per year.[3]

A worker with youth and children (or adults, for that matter) needs to take seriously any suicide threat that a child or teenager makes. Giffin and Felsenthal do a great service in listing thirteen "deadly myths" about suicide that we need to overcome in order to minister to persons contemplating suicide.

The Deadly Myths

1. Nothing could have stopped her once she decided to kill herself.

2. The person who fails at suicide the first time will eventually succeed.

3. People who talk about killing themselves never do.

4. When people talk about killing themselves, they're just looking for attention. Ignoring them is the best thing to do.

5. Talking about suicide to a troubled person may give the person morbid ideas.

6. People under a psychiatrist's care rarely commit suicide.

7. Suicides often occur out of the blue.

8. People who kill themselves are always insane.

9. Once persons try to kill themselves and fail, the excruciating pain and shame will keep them from trying again.

10. My son was depressed and suicidal. But the depression has lifted. He's so much better and happier. He's finally out of danger.

11. Only a certain type of youngster commits suicide, and my child just isn't the type.

12. Suicides are mainly old people with only a few years left to live.

13. Suicide runs in families, so you can't do much to prevent it.[4]

These are myths. Do not believe them. Those who work with suicide prevention have found that these myths are deadly because they keep people who would like to help but do not know how from realizing that a need exists.

Suicide is a reality—even in Christian families. If a worker-counselor has reason to suspect that someone is considering suicide, that person should be encouraged to seek professional help. However, do not feel that because you do not have expert skill in this area that you should step out of the picture. Most suicides feel that no one wants to be around them. They feel cut off from all friends. As a worker-counselor, you may have the opportunity to establish a relationship that a professional counselor would not have. Refer the person to a professional counselor but stay close and offer support and the opportunity to talk that may help the person pass through the period of depression.

Legal Matters

Matters involving legal decisions are also an occasion to refer. In the case of a divorce or when someone is involved with a criminal situation or any other matter needing legal help, do not hesitate to refer to a lawyer. Lawyers are bound by a rule of confidentiality even as are doctors and counselors. Often, if a person can secure legal help it will eliminate a source of conflict that has caused pain over a long period. If money is a problem, the person can be referred to the Legal Aid Society for free or less expensive legal help.

Chronic Needs

Some needs are of such a nature that they cannot be taken care of quickly or even over a period of several weeks or months. Few worker-counselors would have the kind of time to devote to long-range problems.

Roy was only forty-seven when he began to experience dizziness and occasional blackouts. He went to the doctor who discovered that he needed surgery on the arteries leading to the brain. During this time his Sunday School teacher visited him regularly. When he entered the hospital, the teacher went by the day before surgery and had prayer with Roy.

During the surgery, Roy had a stroke which left him partially paralyzed. He lost most of his ability to speak and could not even feed himself. He needed extensive rehabilitation, and the family needed support and help with some of the bills. This was too much for one person. All of the church became involved as well as the medical community. Some of the short-term needs were provided for immediately, and plans were made to take care of some of the long-term needs as well. The teacher could not have provided this kind of help by himself—regardless of how much he had wanted to do so.

Too Personally Involved

Worker-counselors need to refer when they would become too personally involved. Close friends who are going through marital problems may need to be referred to someone who is not as personally involved. It is not unusual at all to have a couple work through their problems and then to feel embarrassed because they shared too much with someone they see regularly. Hence, they drop out of Sunday School and may even change churches because of the embarrassment.

Persons with Physical Needs

Possibly some word needs to be said about the person in physical need. Many hungry people live in our world. Some of these hungry people live in your area. Some have only recently become that way because they have lost jobs. Others have learned to live that way. Some have even come to like their life-style and have become quite adept at working the system to their advantage. Many families need help in emergency situations. However, few worker-counselors have the ability to provide long-term help to those who have financial needs. This is another situation where worker-counselors need to refer to someone who can provide more help (such as food stamps, job rehabilitation, etc.) and also provide some counseling to help change this kind of life-style.

Each situation of referral is unique. One cannot set up hard-and-fast rules saying when a person should or should not be referred. However, the following general guidelines will offer some help to the worker-counselor.

1. Don't feel guilty about referring to someone who has more skill and can provide better help in the long run.

2. Do not desert persons you have referred. Don't let them feel you have "washed your hands of them." Continue to support them with your presence and prayers.

3. Refer when you do not have the time to handle the situation.

4. Refer when you do not have the skills required to handle the situation.

5. Refer when you may be too emotionally involved in the situation.

6. Refer when someone is sick—mentally or physically.

7. Refer when someone needs legal advice.

8. Always have the person's permission before you share matters of a personal nature with anyone else.

To Whom Do You Refer?

Knowing when to refer is only half of the matter. The other half is knowing to whom to refer. As a Sunday School worker-counselor your first priority of referral should be your pastor. Janice Bell (referred to in chapter 2) referred Natalie to her pastor, Dr. Howard. This should be your first priority unless you have good reasons for it not to be.

Some pastors do not counsel. They do not see this as their role and calling. Even so, it would be good to tell your pastor about many—if not all—situations that you encounter if his knowing would help him to minister to the people involved.

Other pastors are not capable of counseling. This is something they do not do well. Just because a person has been called to preach does not necessarily mean that the counseling gift comes automatically with the call.

Others have tried the pastor and found he has not or cannot help. This is no reflection on the pastor or the people needing help. It is just to say that sometimes people have personalities that keep them from helping. Too, some of the same reasons you should refer (lack of time, ability, or fear of personal involvement) may also be in force with your pastor. Your pastor has the same right to refer that you do.

The rule still stands: *your first priority of referral should be your pastor unless you have good reasons not to refer to him.*

In most communities one has many other resources. A worker-counselor should make the effort to discover what these are. Most communities have a city/county mental health organization. These organizations offer a variety of services. Call and make an appointment to have them explain what services are available to the community and how one goes about securing these services. In most situations you will find that your inquiry will be welcomed.

A chaplain in a local hospital may be able to offer you assistance and serve as a resource person. Make inquiries about doctors who have helped people successfully.

Private counselors, psychologists, and psychiatrists are also available. In most cases a person's insurance policy will cover this kind of help.

To meet the physical needs of people, a worker-counselor should be acquainted with the helping agencies in the community that provide such things as food, shelter, clothing, and jobs. Your church may help in some of these areas, but the more you know what is available in your community, the more you will be able to help those who come to you for help.

Do you have a Legal Aid Society in your area? Do you know a lawyer who would be concerned to provide a ministry as well as to perform legal services?

If you work with youth, it would help for you to know the counselors in the schools. They can provide help for you. What about other pastors in the area? Some of them may be gifted in the counseling area. Help is available in most areas. It takes time to discover it.

How to Make the Referral

Wayne Oates suggests six steps for the pastor to follow in referring people; they would also apply to the worker-counselor.[5]

1. *The first step in the referral is to recognize the need and your limitations to meet the need.* If the problem the worker-counselor is trying to solve is too great or the situation creates a problem for the worker-counselor, then the person should be referred. It is not only all right to ask for help, it is imperative that you ask for help when the needs of the person lie beyond your ability to meet those needs.

2. *Interpret the person's difficulty.* Janice Bell shared with Natalie that she needed more help than Janice could offer and suggested that Natalie see the pastor. Janice affirmed that Natalie did have a problem that required more professional help that she could offer.

3. *Confess your own limitations and express your concern for the health and healing of the person you are helping.* Be careful at this step. Do not say: "There is nothing I can do to help you." That makes the person feel like nothing can be done to solve the problem. Point out what you

can do. By suggesting that she would pray for Natalie, Janice assured Natalie of her concern and her willingness to do all she could to remedy the situation. She was also able to admit that she did not have the skills necessary to help Natalie and her parents.

4. *Put the person in touch with the one to whom you have made the referral.* In Janice's case, she immediately took Natalie to the pastor. This is not always possible. It may involve more than that. The worker-counselor can offer to call and alert the one to whom the referral is being made to expect a call or visit from the person. This helps break down the barriers. However, a worker-counselor should have the permission of the person before such a contact is made. It is probably best to let the person in need make the appointment. Most counselors require that the counselee be the one who makes the appointment. If the person needs immediate help, you might provide transportation to the person to whom you are referring him. At least you can offer to do so.

5. *Express concern for the person being referred.* It is imperative that the person being referred does not get the feeling that you do not want to help. Be honest and forthright about why you are referring. At the same time assure the person you are going to continue to support her with your prayers and visits.

6. *Follow up on your promise.* Be certain that you back up your promise with action. If the person has been hospitalized, go by the hospital for a visit. Janice could have called Natalie during the week to see how she was getting along. Sometimes, if the person is at a distance, a note could be sent to communicate a prayer for the person(s) involved.

The ministry of referral is a significant part of the counseling ministry of the Sunday School worker. It, like all other forms of ministry, must be bathed in prayer that the Great Physician will be able to use the particular aspect of the ministry for the person's healing and His glory.

Notes

1. Mary Giffin and Carol Felsenthal, *A Cry for Help* (Garden City, N.Y.: Doubleday and Company, Inc., 1983), p. 39.

2. Ibid, p. 14

3. Ibid.

4. Ibid, p. 17.

5. Wayne E. Oates, *The Christian Pastor* 3rd ed. rev., (Philadelphia: Westminster Press, 1982), pp. 277-83.

Annotated Bibliography

The following books, magazines, and pamphlets are listed to help the Sunday School worker who wants to be a more effective counselor and encourager. Some of the books are intended to be read by the counselor; others can be shared with the person needing help. Some of these books may be in your church media library. Check there, or see if they can be ordered. If not, try your public library, or check with your pastor. Certain ones will become your favorites. These you probably should own, so you can loan them to people.

However, before you loan any book, be sure you have read it and that it fits the situation. Books are not intended to take the place of a personal ministry; they are only a supplement to it.

General

Cole, W. Douglas. *When Families Hurt.* Nashville: Broadman Press, 1979. The book is an encyclopedia of information about numerous topics that the worker-counselor will confront. The forty-nine brief chapters run from abortion to working wives. Each chapter is two to three pages long. The distinct advantage of the book is that it offers a brief response to many problems. Its brevity is also a disadvantage.

Home Life. This quarterly periodical carries articles on all aspects of the home. The articles are inspirational as well as informational.

Ages Birth-5

Living with Preschoolers. This quarterly periodical contains articles for parents who have preschool children or those who work with preschoolers.

Ages 6-11

Dobson, James. *Dare to Discipline.* Wheaton, Ill.: Tyndale House, 1970. Dobson uses a prictical, down-to-earth approach to discipline. The book seeks to answer many questions parents have about discipline.

_____. *The Strong-Willed Child: Birth Through Adolescence.* Wheaton, Ill.: Tyndale House, 1978. The book develops further many of the ideas Dobson expressed in *Dare to Discipline.*

CHANDLER, LINDA S. *David Asks, "Why?"* Nashville: Broadman Press, 1981. Dealing with the pain and grief of divorce is always difficult. This book can be given to a child to read. It can be used as a discussion starter.

_____. *Uncle Ike.* Nashville: Broadman Press, 1981. Children need to grieve at the time of death. Chandler deals with some of the feelings children have at the time of the death of a family member.

Living with Children. A quarterly periodical for parents of children. The articles deal with problems and situations confronted by parents. This is a good magazine to give to parents who need guidance.

Price, Max. "Helping Children Cope." A series of nine pamphlets written for parents and workers with children. The areas covered are illness and hpspitalization, moving, divorce, stress, competition, death, disturbed parents, financial stress, and natural disasters.

SAYLER, MARY HARWELL. *Why Are You Home, Dad?* Nashville: Broadman Press, 1982. How can adults explain unemployment to children? This true-to-life fiction book can be given to a child whose parent is unemployed.

WARD, JEANNETTE W. *I Have a Question, God.* Nashville: Broadman Press, 1981. This book about adoption is one that can be given to a child to read to help explain some of the feelings the child may be having. Read it before you loan it.

Ages 12-17

BOOHER, DIANNA DANIELS. *The Faces of Death.* Nashville: Broadman Press, 1980. This is an excellent book to help youth deal with death. The chapter "When Someone You Love Is Dying" is filled with helpful hints about how to relate to someone who is terminally ill.

CANNON, ANN. *My Home Has One Parent.* Nashville: Broadman Press, 1983. How many problems can a youth living with a single parent face? Are there advantages? This book deals honestly with problems and benefits of a single-parent home.

Living with Teenagers. This quarterly periodical provides articles about teenagers and their families. The articles deal realistically with parent-teenage conflicts.

Suicide

GIFFIN, MARY, AND FELSENTHAL, CAROL. *A Cry for Help.* Garden City, N.J.: Doubleday and Company, 1983. The authors write for parents, alerting them to the warning signals of suicide among children and youth. A final chapter is addressed to "Helping the Survivors."

Death and Grief

BROOKS, D. P. *Dealing with Death—A Christian Perspective.* Nashville: Broadman Press, 1974. The book is an honest and straightforward discussion of death. It is divided into two basic sections. One is practical ("Death Creates Practical Problems"), and one is theological ("Death Raises Ultimate Questions"). Its brevity (126 pp.) is both an advantage and a disadvantage.

CLAYPOOL, JOHN R. *Tracks of a Fellow Struggler: Learning to Handle Grief.* Waco, Tex.: Word Books, 1974. These are sermons preached before and after the pastor's twelve-year-old daughter died of leukemia. The book deals honestly with the feelings of a parent at the sickness and death of a child.

HAVNER, VANCE. *Though I Walk Through the Valley.* Old Tappan, N.J.: Fleming H. Revel, 1974. The author traces his struggles with losing his wife after thirty-three years of marriage.

JOHNSON, L. D. *The Morning After Death.* Nashville: Broadman Press, 1978. Johnson describes his experience in going through the death of his twenty-three-year-old daughter.

MADDEN, MYRON. *Raise the Dead!* Waco, Tex.: Word Books, 1975. The book describes a psychological approach to dealing with death. The book is difficult reading but rewarding.

TUCK, WILLIAM P. *Facing Grief and Death.* Nashville: Broadman Press, 1975. This is an excellent little volume on death. The chapter on "Helping a Friend in Grief" should be read by all Sunday School worker-counselors.

WESTBERG, GRANGER E. *Good Grief.* Philadelphia: Fortress Press, 1972. The author traces ten stages of grief through which we pass. He suggests grief can be caused by loss of a job, divorce, death, or other loss.

Marriage and Divorce

ANDERS, SARAH FRANCES. *Woman Alone: Confident and Creative.* Nashville: Broadman Press, 1976, *o.p.* The book addresses some of the problems a single woman faces in today's society. Although written by a never-married single, the book speaks to the single-again woman, whether through divorce or death.

CROOK, ROGER H. *An Open Book to the Christian Divorcee.* Nashville: Broadman Press, 1974. The book is written to help a person who is contemplating or has already been granted a divorce. It is written from a Christian point of view. Two helpful chapters describe "Your Social Adjustment" and how to relate to "Your Children."

CLINEBELL, HOWARD J. AND CHARLOTTE H. *The Intimate Marriage.* New York:

Harper and Row, 1970. The authors have written a vital book on developing and/or restoring intimacy in a marriage relationship.

TOWNER, JASON. *Jason Loves Jane (but They Got a Divorce)*. Nashville: Impact Books, 1978. An account of a breakup of a marriage and how the man worked through his grief.